Praise for *Spies of No Country*

"Wondrous . . . Compelling . . . Friedman succeeds in portraying the 'stories beneath the stories' that acted as a bedrock to the rise of the Mossad and serve still as a window into Israel's troubled soul." —*The New York Times Book Review*

"An important book . . . Americans are not accustomed to hearing about Israel's complexity, or its diversity. Meaningful opinions require nuanced understanding, and *Spies of No Country* offers that." —NPR.org

"Engaging . . . Illuminating . . . When I was done, I couldn't stop thinking about the men inside the Beirut kiosk, selling candy and pencils to schoolchildren while secretly listening to a transistor radio tucked in the back, trying to pick up news from home." —*The Washington Post*

"One of the most compelling, compulsively readable histories I've read in a long while. Matti Friedman is a lyrical writer and a master of suspenseful storytelling. His gripping spy story doesn't just narrate Israel's heroic founding—it illuminates its tortured present." —Franklin Foer, author of *World Without Mind*

"[An] absolutely arresting account of espionage at the genesis of the Israeli state." —*Booklist*, starred review

"Intriguing . . . Resurrects early operations of the intelligence service of the Palmach, the nascent military that ultimately grew into the mighty Israel Defense Forces." —*The Wall Street Journal*

"*Spies of No Country* is thrilling, moving, and, like everything that Matti Friedman writes, deeply humane."

—Nicole Krauss, author of *Forest Dark*

"A fascinating and dramatic account. *Spies of No Country* is a riveting history." —*The Washington Times*

"Time spent with Friedman's extraordinary book repays the reader's investment tenfold." —*The Federalist*

"A thrilling Israeli spy story . . . Matti Friedman tells this story with great style. Not only is *Spies of No Country* good on such sophisticated, tangled questions of identity; it also just tells a fun story. As a literary document, *Spies of No Country* is exquisite . . . beautiful and exciting." —*The Forward*

"On the surface, it's an engaging spy saga. Beneath that, though, lies an examination of identity and the humanity behind both sides of the ongoing Arab-Israeli conflict."

—*Washington Independent Review of Books*

"Excellent . . . Compelling . . . [The spies'] stories are an unjustly forgotten—and fascinating—aspect of Israel's founding. [Friedman's] deeply researched book is not only enjoyable but groundbreaking."

—*Jewish Review of Books*

"We learn more about what a real-life espionage agent actually does in *Spies of No Country* than in any mere thriller . . . So exotic that it sounds like something out of the imagination of Ian Fleming." —*Jewish Journal* (Los Angeles)

"Compelling." —*The Jerusalem Post*

"Splendid. A noteworthy and authentic spy story. Friedman's account of the Arab Section is an eye-opening narrative of the early days of the State of Israel." —*New York Journal of Books*

"Compelling . . . Thrilling . . . Like the best le Carré. Friedman's superb storytelling skills are such that he employs the devices of fiction, most notably the use of dramatic irony, which gives the narrative a particular poignancy." —*The American Interest*

"Enthralling." —*Commentary* magazine

"Remarkable . . . A fascinating account . . . A wealth of information and various tidbits that make it so worthwhile to read." —*Manhattan Book Review*

"An exquisite account of a thrilling and all-but-forgotten story of the origins of the Israeli spy system . . . [Friedman] shows us how a heroic little band of Jewish spies from Arab countries helps explain the political and cultural transformation of Israel from its European Jewish origins into the largely Middle Eastern country it is today. With *Spies of No Country*, Matti Friedman proves that he is one of the essential interpreters of Israel writing today."
—Yossi Klein Halevi, author of *Letters to My Palestinian Neighbor*

"The author deftly navigates the complicated identities and the stories beneath the stories. An exciting historical journey and highly informative look at the Middle East with Israel as the starting point." —*Kirkus Reviews*

SPIES OF NO COUNTRY

ALSO BY MATTI FRIEDMAN

Pumpkinflowers: A Soldier's Story
of a Forgotten War

The Aleppo Codex: In Pursuit of One
of the World's Most Coveted, Sacred,
and Mysterious Books

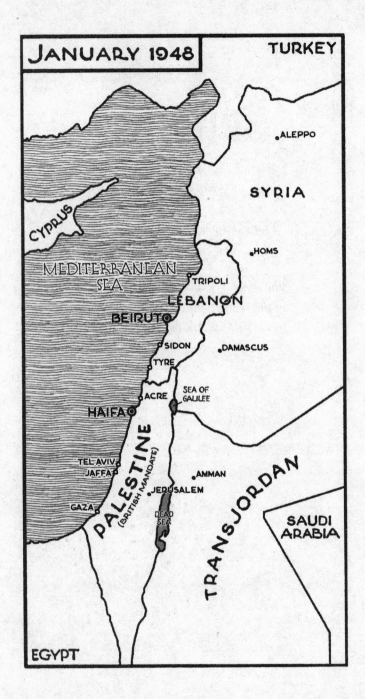

SPIES OF
NO COUNTRY

Israel's Secret Agents at
the Birth of the Mossad

Matti Friedman

ALGONQUIN BOOKS OF CHAPEL HILL 2020

Published by
Algonquin Books of Chapel Hill
Post Office Box 2225
Chapel Hill, North Carolina 27515-2225

a division of
Workman Publishing
225 Varick Street
New York, New York 10014

First paperback edition, Algonquin Books of Chapel Hill, February 2020.
Originally published in hardcover by Algonquin Books of Chapel Hill in
March 2019.
Printed in the United States of America.
Published simultaneously in Canada by Signal, an imprint of
McClelland & Stewart, a division of Penguin Random House Canada Limited,
a Penguin Random House Company.
Design by Steve Godwin.
Map design by Michael Newhouse.

The hardcover edition of this book has been cataloged as follows:
Library of Congress Cataloging-in-Publication Data
Names: Friedman, Matti, author.
Title: Spies of no country : secret lives at the birth of Israel / Matti Friedman.
Description: First edition. | Chapel Hill, North Carolina :
Algonquin Books of Chapel Hill, 2019. | Includes bibliographical references.
Identifiers: LCCN 2018026756 | ISBN 9781616207229 (hardcover : alk. paper)
Subjects: LCSH: Palmach. | Palestine—History—1929–1948. |
Undercover operations—Israel. | Special forces (Military science)—Israel. |
Israel-Arab War, 1948–1949.
Classification: LCC DS126.3 F75 2019 | DDC 327.12095694—dc23
LC record available at https://lccn.loc.gov/2018026756

ISBN 978-1-64375-043-9 (PB)

10 9 8 7 6 5 4 3 2 1
First Paperback Edition

The tropes of espionage—duplicity, betrayal, disguise, clandestinity, secret knowledge, the bluff, the double bluff, unknowingness, bafflement, shifting identity—are no more than the tropes of the life that every human being lives.

—WILLIAM BOYD

CONTENTS

THE SPIES

Gamliel Cohen
Alias: Yussef
Born: Damascus, Syria
Age in January 1948: 25

Isaac Shoshan
Alias: Abdul Karim
Born: Aleppo, Syria
Age: 23

Havakuk Cohen
Alias: Ibrahim
Born: Yemen
Age: 20

Yakuba Cohen
Alias: Jamil
Born: Jerusalem, British Palestine
Age: 23

PREFACE

Of the four spies at the center of this story, only Isaac is still alive. The bespectacled fighter from the alleyways of Aleppo is ninety-three as I write these lines. The suggestion that I meet him came from another pensioner of Israel's intelligence services, a man I knew from working on a different story. I went to see Isaac not because I'd heard of him or of the little outfit to which he'd belonged at the creation of the state, and not because I planned to write this book, but only because I've learned over years as a reporter that time spent with old spies is never time wasted.

I ended up spending many hours over several years speaking with him against a backdrop of olive-green wall tiles in his kitchen, which is on the seventh floor of an apartment block in the metropolitan sprawl south of Tel Aviv. Sometimes he crossed slowly to the stove and brewed black coffee in a little metal pot with a long handle, like the ones they used at the famous campfires. His words were measured; chattiness wasn't a quality these men respected. His memory was a sharp blade. Sometimes it seemed as if the Independence War of 1948 had just ended or was still on.

He laughed more than you'd expect, every few sentences, a deep *heh-heh-heh* accompanied by the shaking of a head that was now mostly ears, nose, and grin. What he laughed at was seldom funny. He wasn't making light of things but expressing wonder at all he'd seen. As he spoke, there were flashes of Isaac as he must have been in those days—watchful, quick, and hungry. He spoke for the others, the ones who survived to old age and died in bed, and the ones who set off with their thin disguises into the storm of events seventy years ago and vanished.

When Isaac first arrived at a vegetable market in Tel Aviv in 1942, a penniless Arabic-speaking teenager squatting on the ground with a crate of peppers, he could have remained there. Many people have arrived at such a market and stayed forever, like my great-grandfather, who sold oranges from a cart on the Lower East Side of Manhattan. But that didn't happen to Isaac. A freak tide lifted him up and carried him away. He could have ended his life at twenty-three among dunes with a bullet in his head, like some of his friends, or hanging in a prison yard, leaving the barest memory of a person. But he slipped through. He could have evaded capture only to have the Jewish state destroyed at its birth in 1948. But that didn't happen either, and here we were in that state, our state, sitting at Isaac's kitchen table.

"Espionage," John le Carré once observed, "is the secret theater of our society." Countries have cover stories and hidden selves, just like their spies, and our clandestine basements conceal insights into the world aboveground. Beyond an affinity for tales of secret agents and double identities, this observation is why I was drawn to these men and their strange adventure. Who they are has something important to tell us about the country they helped create.

The years of my acquaintance with Isaac turned out to be the years of the great Arab collapse and the destruction of Aleppo, the city of his birth and childhood, in the Syrian civil war. We watched it happen from interview to interview. At the time of our first meeting in 2011, Aleppo was peaceful and only the synagogues were empty, as they had been since Isaac's family and the city's Jews fled decades before with the great Jewish exodus from the Arab world. But soon Aleppo's churches were empty and many of the mosques, and much of the great Arab metropolis were in ruins.

We saw people making desperate escapes across the Mediterranean, washing up on Greek beaches, trudging inland with their packs and babies. Throughout the Middle East, the Christians, Zoroastrians, Mandaeans, and Yazidis were going or gone, as well as Sunni Muslims who once lived among Shiites, and Shiites who once lived among Sunnis, and people who think or act differently and don't have a tribe that can protect them. The hatred of people who aren't like you, the idea that something will be solved if only such people can be made to disappear—this sometimes starts with Jews but tends not to end there.

One of my conversations with Isaac took place not in his kitchen but at a mall in his neighborhood, where much of the population has roots in the Islamic world, like Isaac, and like half of the Jews in Israel. On the top floor was a video arcade with flashing blue lights, electronic explosions, and crazed parents driven here by summer vacation and the unbearable stickiness outside. The McDonald's was full, and so was a plastic playground in the atrium. At a shop called Aphrodite, scarlet bras were on sale. A woman in orange-rimmed glasses contemplated a lotto form.

The children of the Jewish quarters of Tunis and Algiers were here in Ray-Bans and running shoes. The Jews of Mosul in northern Iraq were also here—not in Islamic State ditches with their neighbors the Yazidis, but drinking lattes in the air-conditioning, eating kosher McNuggets as their kids howled in Hebrew on the trampolines. These were Israelis, but not the kibbutz pioneers of the old Zionist imagination, orphaned children of Europe. These were people from the Islamic world, in the Islamic world, their lives entwined with the fate of the Islamic world, like the lives of their grandparents' grandparents. This was Israel, but an Israel not visible in the way the country is usually described.

At a chain café by the escalators sat the spy Isaac Shoshan, formerly Zaki Shasho of Aleppo, also known as Abdul Karim Muhammad Sidki of Beirut. When he recounted how he saw Israel born, the story had none of the usual characters and sounded unlike any I'd heard, but explained more about the present than any I'd heard. It was a Middle Eastern story. When I left the mall, the streets themselves seemed different. That's when I decided this was a story whose time had come.

In telling it I've relied on my interviews with Isaac and others; on files from Israel's military archive, including many declassified for the first time at my request; on documents from the archive of the Hagana, the Jewish underground army before the creation of the state; and on unpublished testimonies from participants who died before I could speak with them. Two published histories of the Arab Section—both in Hebrew, never translated, and now out of print—proved especially useful. The first, by the historian Zvika Dror, was published in 1986 by Israel's Defense Ministry, and for simplicity's sake I'll call it the official history. The second was written by one of our four agents, Gamliel Cohen, at the end of his life, and published in 2001. Quotes from documents, recordings, or my own interviews appear in quotation marks. Quotes summoned from memory appear without quotation marks. Notes on sources appear at the end.

The unwritten rules of espionage writing seem to require a claim that the subjects altered the very course of history, or at least of their war. This is tempting but rarely true, I suspect, and it isn't true in the case of our spies, though their contribution to the war was significant. Their mission didn't culminate in a dramatic explosion that averted disaster, or in the solution of a devious puzzle. Their importance to history lies instead in what they turned out to be—the embryo of one of the world's most formidable intelligence services, "a modest beginning for a long and fruitful tradition," in the words of the historians Benny Morris and Ian Black, "a direct link between the amateurish, small-scale beginnings of Zionist intelligence work and the larger, more professional efforts made after 1948."

In Israeli intelligence, as Dror wrote in his official history, "they learn that the nucleus of the way we conduct espionage begins with 'The Dawn,' the unit that served as the foundation for great operations and from which grew all that became known worldwide years later as the 'exploits of the Mossad.'" Those exploits are useful myths for a small country in a precarious position, because they conceal the frailty of the people behind the curtain. But in our story we have only the people and their frailty, and no curtain.

This isn't a comprehensive history of the birth of Israel or Israeli intelligence, or even of the unit in question. It centers on a period of twenty pivotal months, from January 1948 through August of the following year; on two Levantine port cities eighty miles apart, Haifa and Beirut; and on four young people drawn from the margins into the center of events. I was looking less for the sweep of history than for its human heart, and found it at these coordinates.

PART I

Haifa

1: The Scout

Ayoung man in a new suit crossed a street with a real passport and a fake name. This was in the first month of 1948, the rainy season in Haifa—Mount Carmel rising behind the port in one shade of green, the Mediterranean stretching off in another, the sky low and gray above them both. The man carried a suitcase and moved with intent. His flight left shortly. His dress and manner suggested he wasn't a worker, but was no professor either, perhaps the son of a shopkeeper in an Arab city, which indeed he was. He was calling himself Yussef, so let's call him that for now.

The young man tried to look purposeful, but his composure was a bluff, like his name. He needed to pick up a ticket and get to the small airport outside town, that was all, but he knew he might not make it. The war was barely six weeks old, but the distance between alive and dead had already become negligible—the length of an incorrect verb, an inconsistent reply to a sharp question. Or it could be a detail of dress—a villager wearing shoes better suited to a clerk, for example, or a worker whose shirt was too clean. There was a new and hazardous electricity on the street, a fear of spies and saboteurs. On the walls that Yussef passed were posters put up by the Arab National Council that began like this:

To the noble Arab public:
Beware the fifth column!

Another read:

Noble Arabs!
The National Council is sparing no effort to fulfill its obligations to you, and understands the size of the responsibility it carries on the road to saving the homeland and liberating it from all enemies.

In the archives there's a photograph of Yussef that will help us imagine the scene:

Haifa was the main port of British Palestine, half-Jewish and half-Arab and less a coherent whole than a collection of neighborhoods beginning at the docks and climbing up the Carmel slopes, linked by winding roads and stone staircases—Arabs by the water, Jews up the hill. Unlike Jerusalem, which drew most attention and sentiment, Haifa wasn't a city of disputed holy sites but a practical place with a refinery, warehouses, and the hustlers and furtive activities usually found around ports. You heard not only Hebrew, English, and dialects of Arabic but Greek, Turkish, Yiddish, and Russian. The Union Jack still flew over the docks, as it had since the British conquest three decades before. But now everything was breaking down.

As Yussef walked toward the travel agent's shop to collect his ticket out of Haifa and out of the country, the normal bustle was subdued, the Arab streets bleary and tense. There had been sniping all night along the new barbed-wire line dividing the Jewish and Arab sectors, and people were frightened. The preceding weeks had seen a bloody operation by Jewish fighters in a nearby neighborhood of Arab refinery workers, a reprisal for the killing of Jewish refinery workers by their Arab coworkers, triggered by a Jewish bombing at an Arab bus stop outside the refinery, a reprisal for—you could be forgiven for losing track. There had always been free movement between different neighborhoods in Haifa, but now you couldn't be caught on the wrong side of the line.

Looking at these events from our own times, we understand that these are the early weeks of a conflict that will come to be known as Israel's Independence War, or the 1948 war, and that the Arabs will call "the catastrophe." In early 1947 the British had announced their impending withdrawal from Palestine, their energies and coffers sapped by the world war that had just ended, their willpower broken by the impossibility of governing two peoples hostile to Britain and to each other. In a dramatic vote in New York at the end of that year, on November 29, the United Nations resolved that after the British Mandate for Palestine ended the following summer, the country should be partitioned into two states, one for Jews and one for Arabs. The Jews had rejoiced like drowning people thrown a plank, the Arab world responded with the fury of a civilization dealt one humiliation too many, and the morning after the vote the war began.

It might seem that events are flowing inevitably toward the history we've learned and the present that is familiar to us, but on the day Yussef appeared in Haifa in the middle of January 1948, nothing was inevitable, and no one knew anything yet. There was no state called Israel, nor did it seem likely there would be one. The United Nations had no way to enforce the partition plan. British soldiers and police were still in evidence on the streets, and the Royal Navy blockade in the Mediterranean was still keeping out weapons and Jewish refugees to placate the Arab public. But British power was fading as the pullout approached, and it was replaced by a civil war between Jews and Arabs. There had been waves of violence before, but this time the decisive collision had arrived. The result would be a catastrophe—that seemed clear. But it wasn't yet clear for whom.

I have been to Haifa many times, and have walked around the old neighborhoods trying to summon the life of the place as Yussef would have seen it. The Great Mosque, which once drew masses to the carpeted room beneath its Ottoman clock tower, huddles by a vast new tower of curved and gleaming glass. The graceful stone buildings are outdone by the giant cranes of the modern port. The streets where Yussef walked are still there, and still lively, but now they have different names. Photographs from the 1940s show black-and-white rows of shops, workers in caps and baggy slacks, and British soldiers, but that's just what it looked like, not what it felt like. The people who matter in a city, ordinary people going about their daily business, tend not to see themselves or their business as worth documenting, and leave few traces.

One place that does preserve a record of Arab Haifa is the archive of the Hagana, the Jews' military underground in the years before the Independence War. The Hagana had an intelligence office called the Information Service, whose officers kept tabs on the Arab part of the city, and whose idea of what constituted intelligence seems to have been broad. They collected interesting bits of human detail, organizing the information on pages of typed Hebrew that now occupy dozens of cardboard boxes and brown folders in a lovely old building off Rothschild Boulevard in Tel Aviv.

Thanks to these files it is possible to imagine the streets as Yussef would have seen them in January 1948, the grimy workers' hangouts near the port where "the shouts of the waiters and curses of the card-players mix with the ear-curdling song of the radio," the beggars "reading passages from the Quran and bestowing blessings on passers-by," the energetic crush of people in the markets, the beckoning women in their doorways on the street of brothels, the more genteel spots farther inland, away from the docks. If you were looking for a café—if you wanted some political talk, for example, or hashish, or black-market weapons—you could consider these options:

- Kaukab el-Sabah, or "Morning Star," at 28 Kings Street, run by Kassem Jaber, a Muslim, "a regular meeting place for riffraff." Offers music and alcohol.

- Café George, 1 Allenby Street, run by a Christian, Fadul Jamil Kawar. A meeting place for nationalist activists and political movers.
- Windsor Café, owned by Charles Butaji, who donated money to buy weapons during the Arab revolt of the late 1930s.
- Café Farid, 28 Wadi Salib Street, owned by Farid Shaaban el-Haj Ahmad, an avid supporter of the Muslim hardliners led by the Mufti of Jerusalem.
- A café (no name given) owned by one George Schutz, at 28 Carmel Boulevard. Schutz is a Swiss citizen suspected of spying for the Germans and Italians. His wife is a Jewish Hungarian named Rozhitza, a convert to Christianity, and the establishment is "the scene of regular anti-Zionist propaganda."
- An establishment run by a widow named Badiyeh, popular with British policemen and with "veiled women whose qualities and intentions are difficult to discern."

When at last Yussef succeeded in reaching the travel agent's shop without attracting notice, the day's first twist awaited him: No one was there, and the shop was shuttered and dark. Many of the nearby stores were closed, he saw, the proprietors too scared to leave home after the shooting of the previous night. He needed the plane ticket, so there was nothing to do but wait. But as he did, standing by his suitcase on the sidewalk, a young man strode up and confronted him in Arabic: Where are you from?

From Jerusalem, Yussef replied, using the Arabic name for the city: Al-Quds. He said he was waiting for the travel agency to open.

No, said the other man, staring at him. I don't think you are.

Something about Yussef was off. He was affecting the accent of a Jerusalem Arab and maybe his native dialect was showing through. Or maybe it was the way he looked. But the most dangerous move would be to run, so he parried the questions as best he could until the suspicious man stalked off around a corner, unsatisfied.

That man was quickly replaced by a second, one of the vendors who roamed the streets of Arab Haifa selling little glasses of black coffee. The peddler seemed friendly. Listen, he whispered to Yussef. There are people plotting to kill you. Leave.

The store behind Yussef was still closed. There was no sign of the travel agent.

You have no idea what's going on here, said the peddler. Everyone is his own master, the judge, the hangman. They do whatever they want and there's nothing to stop them.

This was how things turned against you, as if you were a swimmer whose leg is gripped by an anklet of current that tightens the more you fight until it pulls you down. You had to stay calm and believe your lie. The stakes were newly clear to Yussef. They existed in his mind in human form—faces he'd recently seen speaking and laughing, but whose nature had now changed, assuming an ominous cast, becoming illustrations of his fate if he slipped.

Three weeks earlier a Hagana team tapping Arab phone lines recorded an urgent conversation between two members of the Arab militia in the city of Jaffa. This was December 20, 1947, the twenty-first day of the war, at 3:15 p.m.:

FAYAD: I'm sending you two young men suspected of being Iraqi Jews. Question them and decide what to do.

ABDUL MALEK: They've already reached me. It's hard to say whether they're Jews—they speak good Arabic. I particularly suspect the skinny one. I told them to confess, and he washed his face incorrectly. They'll remain here until we clarify their identity.

The militia had seized two suspects, a pair of young men dressed like laborers. They spoke Arabic with Iraqi accents, but that wasn't rare; British Palestine was full of workers from elsewhere in the Arab world. They looked like hundreds of others on the street. Their mistake seems to have been placing a call from a local Arab post office to a number in the adjacent Jewish city of Tel Aviv, an unusual communication across the ethnic line. The call drew the attention of an Arab spy at the telephone exchange, the spy tipped off the militia, and by midafternoon they were under interrogation.

To test their identity, the militiaman Abdul Malek had ordered the suspects to perform the ritual washing before Islamic prayer, something any Muslim would know: hands, mouth, nostrils, face. One of them couldn't do it properly. But the two were insisting they were Muslims, and speaking native Arabic, and it still wasn't clear whether they were Arabs or Jews. A second conversation was intercepted at 6:45 p.m.:

ABDUL MALEK: Regarding the two young men—take them to the hotel and put them in separate rooms. There must be someone there who speaks Hebrew. This person should lie down in the same room as one of the young men, and late at night he should begin speaking Hebrew with him. If he's a Jew he'll answer in Hebrew in his sleep. The same should be done with the other one in the second room.

ABDULLAH: That's a good idea. We'll do it.

ABDUL MALEK: What are they doing now?

ABDULLAH: They're crying, and seem hungry.

ABDUL MALEK: We need to bring them food until we know who they are.

Maybe one of the young Arabs did speak Hebrew in his sleep, or maybe they broke some other way. We don't know what happened next, only what happened last: the militiamen killed one of them with a gunshot and the other with a blow to the head, then buried them together in some dunes outside town. It would be three decades before they were discovered by construction workers, and nearly six before they were identified in 2004 as Gideon and David, both twenty-one years old.

Two days after the pair was seized in Jaffa, on December 22, an itinerant nineteen-year-old peddler was seized in similar circumstances near the town of Lod. His executioners hid the body so well it was never found. Then a fourth imposter was caught near Jaffa, and this time it made the press: On December 24 the Arab newspaper *Al-Shaab* reported that militiamen had caught a Jew who spoke Arabic and claimed to be a barber, and who tried to prove he was Muslim by reciting the ritual formula known as the *shahada*, testifying that God is one and that Muhammad is his prophet. They were about to shoot him in a grove of trees, but he was spared when they hesitated and turned him over instead to the British police. Within four days, four had been caught and three killed. Anyone connecting the dots on the Arab side could see the Jews had some kind of ruse afoot.

In Haifa three weeks later, after the suspicious man's questions and the coffee vendor's warning, Yussef knew he needed to get off the street. He was the scout, so he'd been told. They said he was worth a whole battalion of infantry. But he hadn't even managed to get out of Haifa yet. He followed the coffee vendor to a nearby butcher's shop. When he went through the door, he saw the butcher was Christian—there was pork inside, and an icebox with beer, both forbidden by Islam.

Please sit, said the butcher. Tell me who you are.

He showed the passport with the name Yussef el-Hamed. He said he was rushing to catch a flight out of Palestine. Things were disintegrating as the British lost control, and soon all the borders would be closed, but passenger planes were still flying from the city's modest terminal.

The butcher dialed a number on the phone in his shop. Yussef understood that it was the travel agent on the line, that he was at home and wouldn't be coming to work because the streets were too perilous. But the travel agent confirmed Yussef's reservation and suggested he go straight to the airport and collect the ticket there. That seemed to solve the problem, but just as the butcher hung up, the man who had accosted Yussef on the street appeared in the shop with an accomplice. They'd come for him, and they meant him harm.

The accomplice gestured at Yussef. Ah, this guy, he told the first man. Leave him alone, I know him from——. He identified Yussef as being from a certain Arab town.

Yussef spotted the trick. He was supposed to agree in relief, forgetting that it contradicted his story about being from Jerusalem.

I don't know either of you, he said. I'm from Jerusalem, just passing through.

The two men ordered him to come outside, but the butcher interrupted: the young stranger was in his store and under his protection.

He's coming outside even if you don't want him to, by force, said the first man, drawing a pistol. The butcher drew his own pistol and told Yussef to hide behind the icebox. Then more people showed up in the shop, people who didn't want any trouble, and they pulled everyone apart. The two men disappeared, this time for good. Yussef never knew what tipped them off.

The butcher, his savior, called a taxi and waited with him at a nearby café to make sure he got out safely. A third man joined them at the table.

They were his guests, Yussef said, understanding that an act of generosity and gratitude was called for. What would they have to drink?

The new man, who was Muslim, explained that ordinarily he wouldn't drink alcohol. But this morning, he said, he'd make an exception and have a glass of beer because of the thirty-five Jews.

Yussef hadn't heard the news and wasn't sure what this man meant. There had been a new Arab victory, or so people were saying, near a besieged Jewish enclave south of Jerusalem. Of thirty-five Jewish fighters, not one survived, said the man, grinning, and Yussef made sure to seem as happy as everyone else, though he didn't believe it. Later he discovered it was true. A platoon trying to relieve the enclave had walked into an ambush. One of the fighters was Sabari, a seventeen-year-old Yemeni kid who'd trained with him and the others but hadn't lasted, and transferred to a regular unit.

All the talk at the café was of the war, which was still in its first stage, a civil war inside Palestine fought by Jewish and Arab irregulars. The second stage, the invasion of regular Arab armies, would begin in four months, after the British pullout. But the Jews were already outnumbered and many of their settlements cut off.

The Arab village militias were in action, the Mufti of Jerusalem orchestrating the offensive, the famous commander Abd el-Qader el-Husseini pursuing the Jews with his armed detachment, the Holy Jihad. The best outfit on the Jewish side, the elite Hagana force known as the Palmach, was hemorrhaging men and women around isolated settlements in Galilee and along the treacherous road from the coastal plain up to Jerusalem. The bravest young people among the Jews were strewn among boulders and burned inside their armored trucks. The British general staff, examining the opposing forces, was predicting an Arab victory. Yussef bought a drink for the butcher and the grinning man, and they all drank together until the taxi came.

When Yussef finally reached the airfield, he walked into the terminal and stood at the ticket counter. He'd nearly done it. But now a man in line turned around and looked right at him, and Yussef felt sick. The man was a Syrian Jew who knew him. He knew him not as Yussef, a Palestinian Muslim from Jerusalem, but as a twenty-five-year-old Jew from Damascus named Gamliel Cohen.

Gamliel/Yussef's head felt light, and the scene in the small terminal began to blur and seem unreal. In his confused state he just ignored the man, pretending he'd never seen him before. He didn't know what else to do. On the plane, Gamliel/Yussef sat in the rear, as far as possible from this new threat. Half an hour later the plane thumped and lurched, and the propellers stuttered and were still. When he looked through the oval of glass, he saw Beirut.

He escaped in a taxi as fast as he could, leaving the familiar man behind him, coming through the jumble of buildings, boulevards, and streetcars vying for the plateau between Mount Lebanon and Saint George Bay, stopping not far from the navel of downtown where the streets radiate from the Place de l'Étoile.

I was in Beirut only once, in 2002, traveling on a neutral passport, arriving in the city center the same way, in a cab from the airport in the southern suburbs. I spent a few days exploring the elegant streets with their cafés, and the poor streets with small garages and posters of clerics. The energy of the place reminded me of Tel Aviv—the same sunlit bonhomie, impatience, and swagger, the same worship of life and flesh touched with fear of imminent doom, the same kind of people squeezed between the Islamic interior and the Mediterranean, sweating on a strip of sand between blocky buildings and the water. When I picture Beirut at the time of our story, I imagine that some of this was true back then.

In the Lebanese capital, the government, newly independent of French colonial rule, functioned sporadically. The city's inhabitants were a jumble of Arabic-speaking Christians with an affinity for France, Sunni Muslims with an affinity for Syria, poor Shiite migrants from the countryside, Armenians, Greeks, with overlap among the parts and many shades in between. There were Communists, Arab nationalists, capitalists, hedonists, and Islamists of every stripe. There were plenty of strangers with vague accents and backgrounds. The nervous young man in his new suit was just one more.

He was to communicate by mailing letters in Arabic to P.O. Box 2200, Haifa, addressed to "my friend Isma'il." The border between Lebanon and Palestine was still open and the post functioning, and this crude setup was the best they could do. He had been given little money and was used to staying in the kind of workers' hostel where you shared a room with others. But here he paid a bit more and stayed alone. You never knew what you might say in your sleep, or in which language.

. . .

THIS FIRST FORAY ended up being brief—a month spent alone, marveling at the boulevards and tramline left by the French, at the absence of the gunfire and explosions to which he'd become accustomed at home. Beirut was just eighty miles up the coast from Haifa but oblivious to the growing war in the country to the south; obliviousness was one of Beirut's most salient qualities. He tried to communicate as he'd been told, but when several letters to "my friend Isma'il" went unanswered, he traveled south overland, crossing the border back into Palestine. He would have to make contact in person and get more detailed instructions, and also more money.

Upon reaching the Jewish city of Tel Aviv, he found that people were even more nervous than they'd been upon his departure a month before. For the Jews the terror now was truck bombs. The day that Gamliel/Yussef made it to Tel Aviv was around the time that Arab sappers from the Holy Jihad detonated stolen British army trucks in downtown Jerusalem, flattening buildings and killing nearly sixty people. Among Jews the fear of Arabs was worse than ever.

Gamliel/Yussef was in a small park on a Tel Aviv street with Bauhaus buildings and Hebrew signs, sitting on a bench next to a young woman who'd just asked him the time, when two men jumped him from either side. They tore him from the bench, shoved him into a waiting car, forced his head to the seat, and blindfolded him. He felt the hard jab of a pistol in his waist. He protested in Hebrew, but they wouldn't listen. There were Arabs who knew Hebrew.

He was sweating in his suit—the day was unseasonably warm, and they kept the car windows sealed. They drove around until he lost all sense of direction, and it was a miserable hour and a half before they finally stopped, opened the door, and stood him on his feet. He was near the beach at 123 Hayarkon Street, where the Sheraton Hotel stands in our own time, but the blindfold was still on, so that became clear only later. His captors rushed him down a flight of stairs, stopped, then pushed him through a door. When the blindfold came off, he spat *kus emek*, an Arabic curse so vile and satisfying that it had been adopted in Hebrew and worked equally well among Jews and Arabs.

The first thing Gamliel saw was the grinning face of a Palmach commander he knew. There were a few other men who weren't familiar, but Gamliel recognized the kind of apartment he was in, the kind with unwashed tea glasses, weeks of cigarette smoke, Hebrew newspapers, and weapons hidden in closets. It was one of the hideouts where Jewish underground leaders were running the war and evading British police. He straightened his clothes and tried to recover his cool.

The commander turned to the two thugs who brought the suspect in: They'd made a mistake, he said, laughing. This wasn't the enemy. It was the Arab Section.

2: At Camp

Having nearly been outed by an Arab observer who suspected he wasn't really an Arab, then recognized by a Jew who knew he was a Jew, then nabbed by Jews who thought he was an Arab, the agent finally made it back to his friends. They were camped at a kibbutz on the formerly malarial flatlands of the coastal plain, a cluster of tents and sheds around a water tower. The Section moved around, but the camps looked more or less the same:

This was where they slept on mattresses they sometimes stuffed with corn husks, and where they kept the disguises purchased in the Jaffa flea markets: *keffiyeh* headdresses for villagers, work shirts or cheap *franji* suits, the kind worn by both Arabs and Jews, if they didn't want to draw attention on either side of the line. The chances of a British raid against the Jewish underground were lower now that the pullout was close, but the weapons cache was concealed just in case.

Sam'an the teacher was there, with his English manners and his little Arabic library, and around him the lost boys he'd collected from slums, communal farms, and regular Palmach units, where they stood out among the Jews from eastern Europe because of the wrong skin shade and accent. Most of them didn't have parents in the country, and some didn't have parents at all. Their family was the Arab Section.

Isaac was there, and Yakuba, and Havakuk. With the newly returned Gamliel, these are our four. Three of them—all but Isaac—happened to share the same family name, Cohen, but it's a common one among Jews, and they came not just from different families but from different countries. I've chosen to write about them because they were the agents who took part, individually or together, in the key events of the war; because they left the richest recollections and observations; and because each is compelling, and each in a different way. Havakuk, born in Yemen, was gentle—a quiet watcher. Isaac, the janitor's son from Aleppo, had the muscles of a small boy who'd decided he wouldn't be bullied, and the determination of someone who'd come a long way uphill. Yakuba, raised on the streets around the vegetable market in Jewish Jerusalem, was volatile and unusually brave. Gamliel was cautious and the most intellectually inclined, the only one who'd finished high school.

Among the other men at camp was David, nicknamed Dahud, who already had a wife, and who would soon have a daughter but would never meet her; and Ezra, who provided comic relief and was known for asking his comrades to train him to withstand torture by beating him. One story has Ezra squeezing his own testicles and screaming, "I won't tell, I won't tell!" They used to roll with laughter but wouldn't have if they'd known his fate. There was a pair of younger trainees from Damascus, Rika the saboteur and his redheaded friend Bokai, both with roles to play later on, one heroic and one tragic.

Rika later described what it was like to arrive in this odd corner of the Jewish military underground:

> An old gramophone turned out to be responsible for the noisy Arab tune that echoed around the place. It was balanced on a chair of doubtful stability. Two ill-dressed young men had positioned themselves on sloping ground, each on one side of a backgammon board, and fixed their eyes on the dice as they shouted the numbers. Hebrew and Arabic mixed in the air. A few "intellectuals" sat in a "quiet" corner reading an Arabic newspaper. . . . There was no doubt about it: we were in the camp of the Palmach's Arab Section, that is, the "Black Section."

The men sometimes called it that, the Black Section, because among the eastern European Jews who filled the ranks of the Palmach, and who made up most of the Jewish population in Palestine at the time, Jews from the Middle East were sometimes called blacks. The amount of humor in the unit's name is hard to gauge from the present, but even back then someone seems to have had misgivings. The Hebrew word for "black," *shachor*, was replaced with the nearly identical word *shachar*, meaning "dawn."

That's how the unit became officially known as the Dawn Section, or just The Dawn, the name that appears in many of the spies' typed reports and, when they began moving beyond the border, in the log of coded radio traffic. But the unit was most often called the Arab Section, and that's the name I'll use.

Some surprise greeted Gamliel's appearance at camp, because his letters from Beirut hadn't arrived and they'd feared he'd been caught, that the number of dead had risen to four. The Section was already braced for it, and not just the Section: in those dark weeks at the beginning of the Independence War there was death in every unit of the Palmach and throughout the country, as the hopeful little world the Jews called the Land of Israel was strangled.*

---

* Like most characters in this story, the country in question has multiple names. Palestine was the one used by the British during their rule from 1917 to 1948. Some Arab residents used the same name—Filastin in Arabic—though many rejected the borders imposed by Western powers and saw themselves as part of a greater Arab or Muslim entity. The Jews knew the country as the Land of Israel, or simply the Land. The term "Palestinians" for the Arabs of Palestine came into use only later, like the term "Israelis," and here I'll refer to everyone the way they referred to themselves at the time—as Arabs and Jews.

Gamliel and the others had learned the trade in the quieter years before the war. They slipped in and out of Arab towns around Palestine, practiced dialect, saw what fooled people and what didn't, and collected bits and pieces for the Hagana's Information Service as the Jews prepared for the fight that their more insightful leaders knew was coming. The agents would sometimes bring back nuggets of military value, like a description of an armed rally in the town of Nablus and a quote from an Arab militia leader who addressed the crowd:

> Independence is not given but taken by force, and we must prove to the world that we can achieve our independence with our own hands!

Sometimes it was impressions of Arab society or soundings of the mood, the kind of material sought by Mass Observation in Britain during the Second World War, when citizen-spies reported conversations and rumors to help gauge the direction of public opinion. A Section agent might deliver a summary of a sermon he'd heard at a village mosque during communal prayers on a Friday:

> The sermon didn't include a single sentence about politics. It was about giving charity and tithes to the poor from the yearly harvest.

Or a note on the popularity of the Egyptian movie musical *The Adventures of Antar and Abla*:

> This movie has left a deep impression in their hearts, and songs from the movie are on everyone's lips.

Or a snapshot from a strike called by Haifa's Arab leadership against Jewish political aspirations in the summer of 1947, a few months before the Independence War broke out:

I saw a group of twenty or thirty kids, with six "leaders" about twenty-five or thirty years of age, walking around the neighborhood shouting, "Whoever opens his store is a pimp." I walked for about an hour and a half, and every time a Jewish bus passed they smacked it with sticks. When it was some distance away they threw stones and broke a few windows. The leaders tried to prevent this vandalism. When the group reached the corner of Lucas Street and Mountain Way they saw an armored police vehicle and scattered in all directions.

Sometimes they came back with material that wasn't intelligence at all. The teacher Sam'an took an interest in Arabic proverbs, for example, and told the men to collect as many as they could, rewarding a particularly good one with a bottle of soda or a morning off. This became a habit for Isaac, who published a few hundred of them in a little book many years later:

Esh-shab'an ma ya'ref shu fi bi-'alb el-ju'an
The sated man doesn't know what's in the heart of the hungry.

Lama bi'a el-jamal bi-yeketro es-sakakin
When the camel falls, the knives multiply.

This must all have seemed distant and frivolous by the time Gamliel made it back briefly in February 1948; ten weeks into the war, life at camp was unrecognizable. Demands for intelligence were coming from the beleaguered Jewish forces faster than the surviving men could handle. They were scrambling to grasp the direction of events, delivering reports like this one from Jaffa:

> Private car no. 6544 is in the service of the [Arab] National Council. . . .
>
> Pamphlets were given out to adults forbidding children under fifteen from going outside during the strike.
>
> In the Manshiyeh neighborhood, families are leaving with their possessions.
>
> In a conversation with an Arab man he expressed his opinion that violence is coming.
>
> On Salameh Street at 19:00, there were twenty-five young men in khaki divided into five teams of five.

Between those terse lines it's possible to picture one of the men sitting at a cheap café or smoking on the steps of the post office, looking around, asking a question of a passerby as casually as possible: What do you think—will there be more blood?

Gamliel didn't linger at camp after his return, and he soon disappeared again for good. The remaining men seem not to have paid their comrade much thought once he was gone. It would be a few months before Beirut became the center of the action, and it's not clear they even knew he was there; the unit was too disorganized for real compartmentalization, but you were supposed to keep your missions and alias to yourself. Events inside Palestine were grave and deteriorating, and the rest of the Arab Section had more urgent concerns. The 1948 war was not a chess game. But if we picture it that way for a moment, then Gamliel was a bishop moved to one corner of the board in the hope that he'd be useful later on.

3: The Garage

Around the time that Gamliel set off back to the Lebanese capital, Isaac was sent just across Haifa, on foot, leaving from a Jewish neighborhood and slipping across the fortified line into the Arab sector. He'd been given an intelligence tip about a shop where Arab fighters were getting their weapons repaired.

He took the identity card giving his name as Abdul Karim and started down Nazareth Street, an industrial drag parallel to the water, by the big Muslim cemetery. The city was full of workers from other places, drawn by the boom around the British port, earning pennies, sleeping rough. No one noticed a short but powerfully built man with a mustache, round glasses, and a laborer's soiled clothes.

Isaac hadn't made it to the shop in question when something else caught his eye. Parked in a garage on Nazareth Street was a truck half-covered in canvas, freshly painted with red crosses, like a British army ambulance. He wondered why someone was painting red crosses on a truck, and why this truck was in an Arab garage. He set aside the original mission and crossed back into the Jewish sector to report. The intelligence men worked their sources and got lucky with a tip far more pressing than the first: the truck he'd seen was being rigged to carry a bomb that would go off at a crowded movie theater in Haifa's Jewish sector, the Cinema Ora, that coming Saturday night.

Isaac went back across for another look. This time he brought Yakuba, who used the name Jamil, and who was the one sent most often when violence was expected. The second agent had grown up with twelve brothers and sisters in Jerusalem, and in grade school he'd been "leader of the blacks," as he described it, meaning the Jewish kids from Middle Eastern families. The opposing side was led by a certain Tobinhaus, son of a driver in the national bus cooperative and thus a member of the European Zionist aristoc-racy. They must have been eleven or so. Tobinhaus was big and Yakuba small, but the leader of the blacks had a few tricks: "I knew how to throw stones, and he didn't. He had two left hands. And I had another good weapon—I would bite." When he was seventeen he joined the Palmach to fight for real. Something of his personal-ity can be glimpsed in this photograph:

יעקובה

When the two agents walked down Nazareth Street in Arab guise, they saw that the Abu Sham garage consisted of a walled-in yard with a single gate. The suspicious truck stood by a shed. They smelled fresh paint and recognized a man standing by the truck as a commander of one of the groups of Arab fighters operating in Haifa. They kept walking.

Saturday was approaching, and the Jewish commanders at city headquarters didn't have much time. In February 1948 they also didn't have aircraft, artillery, or anything that could honestly be called a military unit. Had these existed they couldn't have been used anyway, because the British were still in charge and trying to keep the lid on, and the only way to operate was subterfuge. The commanders decided to blow up the Arab car bomb with a car bomb of their own.

Rigging a bomb wasn't hard. The problem was getting into the Arab sector, then into the garage, then getting away. The job was given to the pair of agents who'd already been there: Yakuba would drive the car with the explosives, and Isaac a getaway car. That plan came with its own flaws, however, first among them the fact that there weren't any cars. At the time, the Arab Section didn't even own a radio. When they needed a camera for one surveillance mission not long before, they'd had to borrow a Minox from a civilian they knew.

There are different accounts of how the cars materialized. In one version cited in the official history, a few of the men stole one they found in a Haifa suburb, but had to return it when the owner turned out to be an angry oil executive with enough clout to get it back. According to Yakuba's version, fighters carjacked a camouflage Dodge belonging to a British officer, released the driver, painted it black, and replaced the plates—but didn't use it when Yakuba pointed out that every policeman in the city would be looking for it. Two other cars were finally found. The first, an Oldsmobile, was requisitioned from a wealthy Jewish resident of the city whose support for his people's military efforts was insufficiently enthusiastic. This was to be the getaway car, so the owner had a chance of getting it back. The other car, the type and source of which are unrecorded, would carry the bomb. If all went well, nothing would be left of it by Saturday afternoon.

Another flaw in the plan was that Isaac, the getaway driver, had never driven a car. In the alleys of Aleppo, even a bicycle was an unimaginable luxury; he'd ridden one for the first time only a few months before. This wasn't allowed to slow things down. Yakuba taught him to drive the Oldsmobile in the streets around the science university in Haifa, the Technion—gears on the first day, steering on the second. Isaac grasped steering but not gears.

Meanwhile, inside the Technion, other fighters were assembling the bomb in one of the classrooms and rigging the second car to explode, after first crashing it into a wall and damaging a headlight. This was to create a plausible excuse for repairs, which was to get them into the garage and then buy them enough time to escape. They didn't have a detonator, but one of the men knew how to improvise one with an ampoule of sulfuric acid and a tube running from the ampoule into a condom. Once the ampoule was broken, it was supposed to take seven minutes for the acid to eat through the condom and ignite a mix of potash and sugar, which would light the fuse running from the front seat to the sacks of explosives in the trunk.

By Friday night, the night before the operation, they'd ruined so many condoms that they had to buy more, but it was the Jewish Sabbath and all the pharmacies were closed. One of the fighters called a pharmacist he knew and begged for condoms, and the pharmacist suggested he just restrain himself, or so the story goes. The pharmacist came around. But the new condoms were a different brand than the ones they'd been using so far, which might explain what happened at the moment of truth.

The team working on the car broke the trunk's handle so it couldn't be opened. If someone—an Arab militiaman at a checkpoint, say, or a suspicious mechanic, or a British soldier on patrol—wanted to search the trunk, they'd have to lower the backrest of the rear seat. If that happened, the bomb was wired to detonate with whoever was in the car. Commanders had decided that this mission would be carried out at any cost. Everyone understood what this meant, though Yakuba didn't grasp it himself until the team gathered at the Technion to see him and Isaac off and he noticed that a few of the others were tearing up.

WHILE THE BOMB was being assembled, Yakuba had been scouting the Arab checkpoints they'd need to cross to get to the garage. There were three. He'd drive up to the guards, waving amiably and speaking Arabic, then drive through, then drive back. The idea was to get them used to seeing him around. The worse the fighting became in those weeks, the trickier it was to cross the lines. "Contact with the Arabs has been severely damaged," wrote one Jewish intelligence officer, meaning Arab informers who used to work with the Information Service. "The contacts were severed by the Arabs, who don't dare maintain them; the roads are closed; Jaffa and Tel Aviv are almost completely separated. Several Arabs linked to us have been caught." Intelligence needs blurry spaces between sides, and those spaces were disappearing.

One effect this had was to make the use of disguise more common, which added to the paranoia. One Jewish intelligence document, noting that Arab fighters were using British military uniforms to cross into Jewish areas, warned: "We must assume that they can also disguise themselves as Jews." This had happened in the past: when the Nazis dropped a sabotage team of Arabs and Germans into Palestine in 1944, one of the Arab agents had cover as an Arabic-speaking Jew.

"Any stranger, even an Arab, who appeared in Jaffa, old Jerusalem, Lod, Ramleh, and other Arab areas, came under suspicion and was followed," the teacher Sam'an wrote in an internal document about the 1948 war's first months. He knew his men weren't ready, and had thought they'd have more time to train. *El-ajleh min esh-shaytan*, the teacher always said, citing the Arabic proverb: Haste is from the devil. *Et-ta'ani min er-rahman*: Patience is from the Merciful One. But the war came, there was no time, and the devil had his way.

On Saturday morning the pair of cars descended from the Jewish sector into the Arab streets of the lower city, Yakuba leading with the bomb, Isaac close to his rear bumper, hands tight on the wheel, staying in first gear because he hadn't figured out the clutch.

At the first checkpoint, on Allenby Street, the guards recognized Yakuba: *Salaam aleikum*, they said, and Yakuba said in Arabic: The other car is with me.

They passed the second checkpoint without incident and then came to the third, where the guard waved them down. Yakuba's tactic was always to speak loudest and speak first. It kept the other side off balance. He leaned out the window.

What are you doing here? he barked at the guard. Where's the guy who was here before?

He went to eat, and I'm here instead, the guard said.

Keep your eyes open, Yakuba ordered, as if he were one of the Arab fighters himself, and he added: The car behind me is one of ours.

They were through. When they reached the garage, Isaac parked outside the gate and Yakuba drove in. There were a few other cars in the yard, and the ambulance still stood where they'd last seen it, by the shed, marked on the side with a bright red cross. Yakuba steered over and had just parked beside it, on the left, when three mechanics appeared and yelled at him to move.

One second, what's wrong? asked Yakuba, getting out of the car and playing for time. He hadn't thought they'd be on him so fast.

The mechanics seemed agitated. They didn't want to listen. Move your car, one shouted.

Just a minute, I want to ask you a question, I have a—

We don't care. Move your car first and then we'll talk.

Yakuba got back into the driver's seat, put the car in reverse, then drove forward and parked to the right of the ambulance. He turned off the engine again and got out. They were yelling but he kept playing dumb, asking for their boss. Was he around? Had he gone to eat? Was there somewhere to eat nearby? This went on for a while. He wasn't going to be able to keep it up for much longer.

Out on the street in the getaway car, Isaac could only imagine what was happening inside. He understood something was wrong. The order was to leave if his partner wasn't back in ten minutes. Ten minutes passed.

The mechanics wanted to know where Yakuba was from, and he said Jaffa, which is what the agents said when they operated in Haifa. In Jaffa they said Haifa. He started yelling, and it wasn't an act, he was scared—scared of getting caught, and scared of failing. Dozens of lives were in the balance. Thanks for nothing, he shouted at the mechanics. Go to hell! Learn some manners! He shouted whatever came into his head.

The mechanics stayed on top of him, and finally he got back into the car and made as if to leave. He didn't know what to do. But then they turned their backs, believing they were rid of him, and that moment was enough. He took pliers from the glove compartment and broke the ampoule. The acid began dripping into the condom. Seven minutes.

He opened the car door one last time. Can I get a glass of water here? he asked. One of the mechanics made an impatient gesture toward a faucet. Yakuba walked over, bypassed the faucet, and hurried through the gate onto the street. The Oldsmobile was still there, the engine running. The Palmach code prized friendship above orders, so Isaac had never considered leaving. He moved over to the passenger's side, because now they were going to need someone who could really drive.

Yakuba slipped behind the wheel, tapped Isaac on the knee, and pressed the gas. They were supposed to have plenty of time, but they'd just begun moving when the ground juddered, a shock wave hit the car, and the air filled with shards. People watching from points higher up the slopes of Mount Carmel thought it looked like an atom bomb going off in the lower city. In the moments of eerie silence that follow a blast that size, the two agents watched the black cloud rise and recede in the rearview mirror.

4: The Watcher (1)

One of the great dramas of that time played out not in the land itself but in the sea to the west, where old freighters and ferries dispatched by the Jewish underground in Europe were trying to run Jewish refugees through the British naval blockade. The British had acceded to Arab anger about Jewish immigration and were stopping the ships, interning their passengers in detention camps on Cyprus and sabotaging them at their ports of origin—the *Vrisi* sunk in the harbor at Genoa, the *Pan Crescent* disabled at Venice.

When one actually made it through to the Palestine coast, Jewish fighters came to get the passengers off the ship and inland before British soldiers came to arrest them. Sometimes the Arab Section men were sent, not as spies but as regular Palmach hands. Gamliel and Yakuba were there when the captain of the *Hannah Senesh* beached her on the rocks off western Galilee late one Christmas Eve, the timing chosen because the British troops in the area were assumed to be too drunk to intervene. They worked for hours getting the 252 passengers ashore, and it must have been a remarkable meeting between the Jews from the refugee ship, who'd never been in the Middle East, and the Jews from the Arab Section, who'd never been out of the Middle East. But they were all too preoccupied for sentiment. Some of the little boats they were using capsized, and two women who had survived the Nazis drowned in the surf between the ship and the Land of Israel. The others split into small groups and slipped away. Yakuba remembered it as a "night of horrors."

The most famous Hebrew writer of the time, Nathan Alterman, immortalized the same night in a poem. He described the young Palmachniks carrying the survivors on their shoulders through the waves, and he mocked the British, celebrating the arrival of this single leaky ship with its emaciated passengers as a great Jewish naval victory, "the nation's Trafalgar." The people on the boats were the source of much of the desperation driving the Jews of Palestine in those days, the members of the Arab Section among them. And they were the source of many of the fears on the Arab side. A poster from the Arab leadership, recorded by a Section agent in Jaffa, warned that these refugees were potent enemies, "people who have seen death and fear nothing."

In the summer before the Independence War, the Royal Navy had intercepted an old American ferry, the *President Warfield*, off the coast of Palestine with forty-five hundred survivors on board—a "floating Auschwitz," in the words of one French paper. The passengers fought the boarding parties with clubs and bottles, and British marines killed three of them and wounded dozens before the ship was brought under control and towed to the Haifa port. The vessel had been renamed *Exodus from Europe 1947*.

Watching from the Haifa docks as the pathetic cargo was unloaded were members of a United Nations commission debating the future of Palestine, accompanied by a retinue of journalists. They saw British soldiers transfer the survivors to three ships that would eventually take them back to Germany. The *Exodus* was remembered as a debacle for the British and as one of the events that pushed the commission to support the creation of a Jewish state.

Also watching that day were laborers from one of the crews employed to scrape rust and barnacles off the hulls of ships. Many of the menial port workers were Syrians from the impoverished Houran region, but this crew was made up of Arabs from Palestine and a few from Egypt. They'd all wake up at five in the morning in their cheap hostels, or on the floors of shops rented out by owners for the night, and reach the port by six to catch their launch. They'd spend the day with the sun grilling them and the sound of hammers ringing in their ears, breaking to eat a lunch of pita, tomato, onion, and some salty cheese, then working into the late afternoon. The excitement of the *Exodus* was a welcome respite from the harsh routine. They stared as the ship limped past them into the harbor.

We know what they saw because one of them, Ibrahim, kept a kind of diary. The workers, he recorded, "are deeply impressed by the stubbornness, energy, and wealth of the Jews." They didn't see a tub full of wretched people whose families had just been murdered, whose prospects were so grim that their best option was a hostile beachhead in the Arab world. Instead they saw a canny move by a powerful opponent. When one of the other workers saw the *Exodus* coming into port, according to Ibrahim's record, the man said in amazement: "Where did the Jews get so much money?"

"The Jews own America," another replied.

After work hours, Ibrahim spent time at a sports club for Arab workers, where he was known as a boxer of some prowess. He was meticulous about recording what he saw at the gym, at the port, and in the poor streets by the docks, even if what he saw had no obvious importance. One day at the Café Victor, for example, he watched as two men were dragged out bleeding—an argument over cards had escalated to blows, and a crowd gathered to egg on the combatants until British policemen arrived to break it up. There was blood on the chairs, he noted, on the table where the cards had been, and on the floor. The word *café* didn't mean a quiet oasis of culture and good coffee. There were places like that serving the middle class, but at the cafés frequented by workers like him the hubbub was barely different from the chaos in the street. The floors were rarely washed, and flies buzzed in the air. Women were scarce here, and if any ventured outside they were veiled, except in the streets where the brothels offered their services, where they sat in doorways and tried to draw you in with calls and gestures of invitation.

You were lucky to get a job at the port, any job at all, but the work was arduous, and what made it harder for Ibrahim was the presence of Jewish workers near the Arab crews. Some of these workers seemed to torment one of Ibrahim's Egyptian friends particularly: "They slapped him around and ripped his clothes," he recorded, "and he accepted all of this with a smile." They were nicer to Ibrahim and the Palestinian Arabs, but Ibrahim once heard them refer to him in Hebrew, which they assumed he didn't understand, as an "unclean beast," and joke about his having lice.

At the sports club, he joined other young Arab men training to box beneath photographs of athletes on the walls. Once, Ibrahim spoke to another member about the growing violence; the political temperature in Palestine was rising, and everyone knew the Arabs were arming themselves and preparing to fight, as were the Jews. But the Jews were cowards, this other member explained to Ibrahim—they ambushed under cover of darkness, while Arabs fought face-to-face. He said he longed for a chance to fight.

Ibrahim asked whether the man thought the Arabs were ready for war, because none of the young people training at the gym seemed to know anything about weapons. "I, for example, don't know how to use a rifle," said Ibrahim.

"I know how to use a rifle," the other man said.

"Who taught you?" asked Ibrahim.

His older cousin had been a soldier in the British army, the man said, and when he came home on leave he let the children play with his gun. And once someone, a friend, came to the sports club with a tommy gun and gave them all a quick lesson.

"But we don't have any guns," said Ibrahim.

"There are enough guns," the other man assured him. "The Najada storerooms are full of guns. The Najada is training and is ready for the Jews." This was the name of an Arab militia, one of the Palmach's opposite numbers.

The conversation ended because the evening's boxing class began, but that weekend Ibrahim went to snoop around the Najada building, which was in a different part of the lower city. It's still there today—three modest stone floors by a main road near the Rushmiyeh Bridge. There's a synagogue there now, and a sign explaining that the building was home to the Arab militia and was also the scene of a battle on the day the city fell. But otherwise it looks precisely as it did when Ibrahim went there seventy years ago.

He got in without difficulty and found backgammon boards and a Ping-Pong table. There was also a notice signed by the local militia commander instructing his officers to arrive at noon the following day, wearing their uniforms. Ibrahim made sure to be there too and saw them, a dozen men who seemed disciplined— clean shaven, their shoes shined. After a brief conference the militiamen split up, heading off into the city in twos and threes. The worker didn't dare follow them after that.

5: Tiger

The Arab part of Haifa, the area close to the waterfront, was divided among Christians and Muslims; wealthy and destitute; political moderates, including a contingent of mild Communists, and people of uncompromising politics and religion. The latter tended to be affiliated with the Mufti of Jerusalem, the Jews' archenemy, who'd spent the Second World War serving the Nazis in hopes that their conquest of the Middle East would rid Palestine of both the British and the Jews. Native families were outnumbered by migrants from elsewhere in Palestine and the Arab world, and as violence grew in 1947 and early 1948, foreign Arab fighters were added to the human mix on the streets of lower Haifa.

Among the city's most influential leaders was a preacher whose full name was Sheikh Muhammad Nimr el-Khatib. In the intelligence files he's known as Nimr, which is "tiger" in Arabic. For clarity's sake, that's the name I'll use. He was a force in the local chapter of the Muslim Brotherhood and an ally of the Mufti. By early 1948 the preacher was busy organizing and arming fighters, and for a time Haifa's militia headquarters operated from his home.

As the British pullout approached and the country became more inflamed, Nimr used the pulpit at the Great Mosque to preach holy war. We know because some of the worshippers seated in rows on the carpet, chins tilted upward toward the speaker at the front, were people who weren't supposed to be there.

The Information Service wanted eyes and ears in the mosques to keep track of what the preachers were saying, which would help gauge the mood on the Arab side and the likelihood of violence. This may have sounded straightforward from the offices where such decisions were made, but it was a long time before any of the agents in the field dared to try it, slipping off their shoes and entering a Muslim house of prayer.

One agent left an account of praying for the first time on a Friday in Jaffa: He was steady at first, he said, but his courage vanished after the first prostration, when he was supposed to stand up with his hands on his knees, then raise his hands, palms out. He was surrounded by seven hundred genuine worshippers. The times were violent, and if something went wrong no one could help him. "As soon as I got to that part," he remembered, "my whole body started shaking, and it took a moment or two until I calmed down and looked at the people around me." No one seemed to notice. The agent got out unscathed, but his name appears only briefly in the records; he may not have been meant for the job.

One of the men who heard Nimr speak was Gamliel, before he left on his mission to Beirut. Nimr was a "fire-and-brimstone inciter," Gamliel recorded, charismatic enough to fill the mosque each time he appeared, a preacher who "spoke very sharply, in strong words, and to great effect." Gamliel, the most cerebral of the four spies, was squeamish about bloodshed and had even extracted an unusual promise from the Section commanders that he'd never have to kill anyone. But he found it hard to sit still with the real worshippers when he heard the calls to attack Jews. Sometimes, dark fantasies came to him in the mosque: If only he had a grenade, he'd think, or any weapon at all. But he was there only to listen.

The spies were aware of the preacher by the summer before the war, when Nimr appears in a five-page report from a Muslim Brotherhood rally. This report too was written by Gamliel. Joining the rally as Yussef, he saw the preacher working the crowd with a few toughs who seemed to be his bodyguards. The speakers who preceded Nimr carried on for some time, the agent recorded, calling on the martial spirit of the Arabs for the coming war, demanding a boycott of Jewish goods. But when Nimr's turn came he was concise, speaking for just seven minutes.

He opened by invoking two names. The first was "the sainted hero Sheikh Izz el-Din"—here, in his report, Gamliel noted raucous applause. Izz el-Din el-Qassam was a revered local jihadi killed in combat with the British a decade before. Much later he became an inspiration for the Islamist group Hamas, which named its military wing and a rocket in his honor. "The second spirit," the preacher went on, "is that of our hero and leader, the brave Muhammad Amin el-Husseini." At the name of the Mufti of Jerusalem, two excited men took out pistols and fired into the air. Nimr ended with a call to boycott "anyone selling land, anyone in contact with Jews, and anyone selling or buying their produce." The rally dispersed at 1:00 p.m.

THE PREACHER LEFT his own account of the war, *From the Fragments of the Catastrophe*, an important document of the time, though largely forgotten today. In its dense and passionate Arabic pages he details his efforts to prepare for military action, organizing defense units and buying weapons. These were in short supply because people were arming themselves independently, driving up the price of rifles and pistols on the black market. He turned to the neighboring Arab states, which had their own arsenals, but they never came up with much more than a few old rifles with ammunition that didn't match.

The preacher hoped to buy guns from British soldiers garrisoned in the city, some of whom were sympathetic to the Arab cause, but he found that the wealthy Arabs who could have paid were already fleeing Haifa with their money to wait out the war somewhere safer. Arab brigands, local and foreign, were terrifying residents, and people began hoarding food. "Every day," he wrote, "many Arabs were buried, and safety deteriorated." Nimr's memoir describes his travails during the fighting in a tone that is often angry and disappointed; it was written afterward, when explanations were required about why things had gone so badly. But in February 1948, things weren't going badly. The Arab side had the upper hand, and the preacher's tone, as the spies heard it, was warlike and confident.

The Jews understood that the port of Haifa was vital and that the crucial moment was close. "If we control Tel Aviv and the cities of the coastal plain we'll remain only a canton, an autonomous area, a ghetto," one newspaper editor wrote not long afterward. "If Haifa is ours we'll be a state." The senior Jewish commanders decided it was time. The military files contain a document consisting of a single page of typed Hebrew under the heading "Operation Starling."

"The mission," it reads: "kill Nimr."

6: Isaac

It was Gamliel, the intellectual, who seems to have spent the most time watching the preacher before Operation Starling, but he'd vanished by the time the assassination order came down. The job of tailing the target was given to Isaac, who slipped across the line, finding his way into the lower city near the port.

In addition to his usual workers' clothes and the identity card with the name Abdul Karim, he took a paper bag of sunflower seeds so he'd have something to do while he watched. He sat on a curb near Nimr's apartment cracking his seeds, a young man on Arab streets again, as if he were still living the life intended for him, as if he'd never run away and transformed himself and changed his name and been recruited by the spies and taken yet another name—as if he'd never left home at all.

We may have come as far as possible without saying more about who our characters were and what they were up to. This book isn't meant to be a history of the entire 1948 war, of the Jews of the Arab world, or of the Jewish enclave in Palestine in those days. Excellent histories already exist. I'll say only what is necessary to allow us to grasp where these spies fit into the fraught moment of Israel's creation and to follow them as they're drawn deeper into the war.

For Isaac there was nothing foreign about the curb of an Arab street. Isaac was a child of such streets, the ones that jerked and ducked through the maze world around the Aleppo Citadel. Through a child's eyes he remembers the harsh life of the *hosh*— the courtyard his family shared with a dozen other families in the Jewish Quarter—the dirt and disease, the terrifying nighttime trips to the outdoor toilet infested with mice. Not all the memories are bad. He remembers Aleppo food—not the tamarind dishes of the rich, but rice and flatbread baked over fires fueled by cow dung sold by Gypsies.

But Isaac was on his knees in Aleppo, that was the truth. He existed on the bottom rung of a community that had historically been defined as second class by Islam, and that lived in the shadow of the Arab majority. An English visitor to the city in 1756 recorded that Jewish men wore beards and the women violet slippers, that they spoke Arabic better than Hebrew, that among Muslims the Jews "are held in still greater contempt than the Christians," and that poor Jews were "of all people the most slovenly and dirty."

The arrival of French colonial rule after the First World War had improved the Jews' lot, but Isaac's father still remembered a time when any Muslim pedestrian could tell a Jew to move aside and walk in the sewage ditch in the center of the street. Isaac's father was a janitor who cleaned one of the Jewish schools and set out the coal braziers that warmed the classrooms in the winter. In Aleppo, "janitor's son" wasn't just a description but a prediction. It was all you needed to know about this child's present and future. A photograph survives from Isaac's bar mitzvah at thirteen, the most important day of his young life. In it you see Isaac with a few of his younger siblings, wearing a white shirt, charity shoes, and no socks:

Isaac's escape began with the arrival at school of an emissary
from the Land of Israel. This emissary was one of the messengers
that the Zionist movement had been sending out to Jewish communities since the turn of the century, organizing young people,
calling them back to the homeland. The visitor brought exciting
information. Isaac and the other children already knew the Bible
verses that described Jerusalem, Bethlehem, and the hills and
valleys of the Land; they had to learn the verses by heart both in
Hebrew, the language of study and prayer, and in Arabic, their
mother tongue. But it was the emissary who revealed to them that
these places were real, not in heaven. He'd seen them himself. You
could walk through stone gates and stand in the holy city. Mount

Tabor, where the prophet Deborah and the general Barak rallied their troops against the Canaanites, was a real hill. You could climb it. This hadn't occurred to Isaac, who'd never been out of Aleppo.

The emissary also told the children about something called a "collective," a way to pool resources and improve your lot. This idea struck Isaac. He couldn't afford a saw, hammer, and nails on his own but thought maybe he and a few friends could buy them together and be a collective of carpenters. This emissary had to watch his words: Zionism was dangerous here, and the position of Jews among Arabs was more fragile than ever. This was around the time in 1941 that Arab mobs in Baghdad, a city where a third of the residents were Jews, murdered nearly two hundred of their Jewish neighbors. Nationalism in Europe made no room for the continent's native Jews and was pushing them to Palestine. The Jewish enclave in Palestine was inflaming Arab nationalism, which made no room for the native Jews of the Arab world and would drive them to Palestine in the end too. Forces beyond their control or understanding were operating on them all, and the emissary chose his words with care.

But Isaac understood. There was a place where Jews and workers could stand up straight, and he was going. He ran away when he was sixteen, or when he thought he was sixteen. Isaac didn't know his real birthday. Later on, an investigation of the log of circumcisions performed by the Aleppo rabbis revealed that he'd always been two years older than he thought. He didn't tell his father he was leaving, and he couldn't tell his mother, who'd died when he was small. For Jews in Europe, the Land of Israel was far away, but it was different for a kid from Aleppo; according to Google Maps, the drive from Aleppo to Haifa today would be nine hours and four minutes. He paid a smuggler and slipped across the border at night.

Back home in the Jewish Quarter, the kids whispered about him, the janitor's son who'd actually done it, who'd run away to join the Zionists. He was a hero.

But in the Land of Israel in 1942, he was crouched on a market street in Tel Aviv selling green peppers from a crate. He bought them by weight early in the morning and sold them by unit throughout the day, pocketing the difference, making just enough to eat, watching this new country at knee level—European dress hems and stockings, patched blue work pants, white robes, British khaki from the Manchester mills.

Tel Aviv was an unformed place barely thirty years old, displaced people filling the streets with their foreign bodies. "The masts on the rooftops then / were like the masts on Columbus's ship," the Hebrew poet Leah Goldberg wrote, "and each crow perched at their tip / proclaimed a different shore." She remembered the sound of German and Russian under the fierce sun, "the tongue of an alien land / stuck into the heat-wave / like the cold blade of a knife." Had the poet glanced down at Isaac, what would she have seen? A piece of human driftwood awash in the 1940s, one of millions. No alien, but a child of the heat wave. An Arab boy with a green pepper.

At the Formica table in Isaac's kitchen, I tried to get the elderly incarnation of that boy to talk about his first days in the country. The market still exists, and it's still the kind of place where you can imagine a teenage Isaac crouched in a corner with his crate. It's a twenty-minute drive from his apartment. There was something striking about the contrast between that proximity and the fantastic distances he'd traveled in his life since then. Did he ever go there? Sometimes, he said, but he didn't say much else. I think he saw those days only as a prelude to what happened next. He believed his story was about gaining a small amount of power in the world, about becoming the master of his own fate as his people became masters of theirs. He may not have wanted to dwell on how helpless he was at first.

Salvation appeared in the form of a counselor from one of the Zionist youth movements who came around looking for kids like him—new arrivals from Arab countries selling trinkets or getting into trouble. The counselor was a socialist from a Yemeni family. The youth movement had a clubhouse, the kind of place with backgammon boards, maybe a Ping-Pong table, pictures of Theodor Herzl and Karl Marx, copies of *Auto-Emancipation* and *The Jewish State* that may have been brandished dramatically in lectures or ideological debates more than actually read.

That's how Isaac's Zionist consciousness was raised and how he ended up with a group of Syrian boys in orange orchards far from the city, on a kibbutz called Na'an, carrying sacks of fertilizer—not because he had to, but because this was the mission of the Jewish nation reborn on its ancestral soil. This was the life of the *chalutzim*, the pioneers, the vanguard clearing fields, building homes, and creating a country for the Jewish masses who'd follow. The Zionists had a way of spinning humiliation into ideals. They were impoverished? Poverty was exalted. They'd been hounded from their homes in other countries? That was fine—their real home had always been in the Land of Israel, and they were planning to go there anyway. They were refugees? No—pioneers. It was brilliant narrative alchemy, and in that terrible century it saved the Jews from the trap of victimhood and reversed their fate.

Isaac was now part of the story. Or rather Zaki Shasho was, because that was still his name when he began hauling the fertilizer sacks. The fashion in those days was to adopt a new Hebrew name as part of your personal rebirth, the way David Gruen of Płońsk transformed himself into the leader David Ben-Gurion, "son of the lion cub." It was a time of self-invention, and why not? It wasn't as if the past was so great. Names, as Charles Dickens knew, were powerful things: "Home is a name, a word, it is a strong one; stronger than magician ever spoke, or spirit ever answered to, in the strongest conjuration." A new name could transform you and build you a home.

Isaac found a Hebrew word, *shoshan*, that sounded like his old last name. It meant "lily." He would also use his full Hebrew first name, pronounced not in the French fashion common among the Aleppo Jews, *ee-zak* (of which Zaki was the diminutive), or in the Arabic fashion, *ess-hak*, but in the Hebrew of the pioneers, *yeetz-khak*. This was the name not of a slum kid from an Arab city but of a Hebrew fighter or someone from the Bible. And this is who he was two years before the Independence War, when a pair of strangers arrived at the kibbutz seeking his former self.

THE TWO VISITORS were waiting in one of the commune's unadorned rooms when the Syrian boys were sent in and asked to sit on the benches. The boys, dark to begin with, had been darkened further by the fields. They'd grown their hair long in front, in the style of the sabras, the native-born Jews of the Land of Israel. Their Hebrew was still inflected with Arabic, but improving. They sat down.

The visitors seemed old, maybe thirty. One was the teacher Sam'an. The other was Benny Marshak, a legendary character of the time who served the Palmach as a kind of prophet and political officer, a font of inspirational tales and parables in the tradition of the great rabbis, but without God, because the Palmachniks were atheists. On a dark night in the desert, according to one of his stories, a group of Palmach fighters were escaping after a daring operation and came to the bottom of a sheer cliff. They had to get up somehow, and fast, but there was nothing to hold on to—not an outcropping, not a bump, not a weed sprouting from the rock. So what did they do? They grasped *the idea*, and up they went! Many of the stories had this moral.

The boys had heard whispers about the Palmach, which drew most of its men and women from the kibbutz movement. In fact, they learned, if the kibbutz was the elite of Zionism, the Palmach was the elite of the kibbutz. But if you asked about it, you were told to be quiet. The British and Arabs had ears everywhere.

The Palmach was the only full-time fighting force among the part-time volunteers of the Jewish defense underground, the Hagana. *Palmach* was a Hebrew acronym for "strike companies," but the name, like the entire Zionist enterprise of those days, required some imagination. The Palmach wasn't anything a real military would have recognized as "companies." Nonetheless the Jews imagined it to be the vanguard of their army. The young generation of Jews in Palestine "had been raised to believe there was *nothing* they could *not* do," the historian Anita Shapira has written. "Their self-confidence, nurtured by a mixture of ignorance, arrogance, and the daring of youth convinced that they had been born for greatness, ultimately may have been the strongest weapon in the Palmach armory." In the early days that spirit was one of the only weapons.

Today the Palmach is an Israeli myth, the subject of movies, books, and songs. There's a Palmach museum in Tel Aviv. The name evokes a line of young men and women in backpacks and mismatched khaki, strung along a desert wadi in the blue-black light of dawn—not cowering before the majority like their Diaspora parents and grandparents, but on their feet and on the move. They identified with Tito's guerrillas and the Red Army, liked to call themselves partisans, and believed themselves to be leading the Jewish front in the global workers' revolution. They thought that by creating a socialist future in the Land of Israel, they were also liberating the land's Arabs from British imperialism and Arab feudalism, which is touching, and not at all the way the Arabs saw it. They had their own style and their own slang. They weren't just an army but a kind of potent world unto themselves.

Now Marshak, the envoy from this world, stood and faced Isaac and the other boys from Syria. He'd come, he said, because the Jewish people needed volunteers for special jobs. When the Palmach's first commander, Yitzhak Sadeh, spoke to young Jews in Palestine in those days, he sometimes described the present as a great set of scales: on one side their tiny nation, and on the other the vast forces arrayed against them. "Throw yourself on the scales," Sadeh would exhort listeners, "throw yourself with strength and courage." Would the group agree to send volunteers? the Palmach envoy Marshak now asked the boys in the room. The group was everything in those days. It was unthinkable for individuals to decide by themselves.

The group's response was no. They considered themselves to be insufficiently knit together. The kibbutz needed their labor, and even though some of them, like Isaac, had been there for a few years, they were still learning the ways of the Land of Israel. A few of them couldn't even read Hebrew newspapers yet. An ideological argument followed about the value of communal tasks versus national missions. Was military service more important than tilling the fields with one's comrades? Marshak, a veteran of such meetings, no doubt expected this, and we may assume he let the discussion exhaust itself before he rose to drive the nail home.

The corpse of Nazi Germany was still warm, Marshak told the boys, but the next war was already coming. This time it would be a war of survival fought against the entire Arab world. The newcomers from Arab countries were a treasure, he said, and without them the Palmach would fail. Each of them was worth a "battalion of infantry." That phrase recurs in descriptions of the Section and seems to have been something they were told, or told themselves, quite often.

Thus was Isaac drawn into his secret life, a youth with round glasses, a battalion of infantry.

MATS ON THE ground, and a voice calling the faithful: *Hasten to prayer!*

This is a memory from before the Independence War, on a Friday at noon, the time of communal worship in the Islamic world.

God is great. There is no god but Allah. The Arabic words came from the Al-Aqsa Mosque in Jerusalem through a small transistor.

Wudu! said the man at the front of the tent. Ablution.

There was no running water, so the worshippers used their imagination. They took imaginary water into their mouth and spit it out three times. They inhaled it into their nose and expelled it three times. Some had worry beads. They raised their hands to the level of their shoulders, palms out, then placed their right hand over their left atop their solar plexus, following the prayer leader. They kneeled on the mats, pressing their foreheads to the ground. All of this was imprinted so deeply in Isaac's mind that he could go through the *wudu* for me in his kitchen seventy years later—hands, mouth, nostrils, face—and then begin the prayers, as if he'd been at mosque that morning.

Ṣam'an, who was the prayer leader in the tent, was their guide to Arab culture and Islam. A different Palmach instructor came to demonstrate the use of the Sten and Parabellum, teaching them to dismantle and assemble the guns, the tent flaps always down against prying eyes. A third man came for a course on explosives—the characteristics of gelignite and the kind they called soap, the precise amount needed to knock out an electric pole or a bridge. When they could round up a few bullets, they held target practice in a hidden spot outside the kibbutz perimeter. But when it wasn't time for weaponry, they sat on benches around a table in a tent, inclined toward the teacher Ṣam'an, just as Isaac and the other Aleppo schoolchildren had once encircled the rabbi who taught them Torah verses in Hebrew and Arabic.

The Section was a ragged group drawn from the lower rungs of Middle Eastern society, but their teacher was different. He'd grown up in a middle-class Baghdad home with influences of British colonial power and education. As a young man from the Iraqi capital, Ṣam'an looked like this:

In later photographs from the Land of Israel he appears clean shaven and dressed in Palmach khakis, as in this one of him, at the center of a group of trainees:

The teacher was shy, as his pupils described him, and so polite that he was embarrassed to laugh out loud—he would just smile and rock back and forth, his eyes tearing up. Sam'an had a Hebrew name too, but no one used it. The Arabic one fit better. Most Palmach commanders were in their early twenties, and some of the fighters should still have been in high school, but when the Independence War began the teacher was thirty-two, which made him seem ancient. "This was Sam'an," Yakuba remembered, "and we worshipped him more than any other man."

Later on, Sam'an became one of the most respected spymasters in Israeli intelligence. His most famous pupil was also Israel's most famous spy, Eli Cohen, a Jew born in Egypt to a Syrian family, who penetrated the highest levels of the Syrian regime in the early 1960s as a businessman named Kamal Amin Thabet. Cohen was caught and hanged in Damascus in the spring of 1965. We may assume the existence of other pupils of Sam'an whose fates were less bitter and whose names are thus unknown to us. The teacher was discreet throughout his life, and his writing appears only in internal documents. He seems never to have published a word.

The Jewish intelligence service had traditionally relied on networks of paid Arab collaborators willing to work with the Jews for money or for the chance to harm their political enemies. The information was expensive and often unreliable, and operating this way also contradicted the Zionists' ideal of doing everything themselves, from picking oranges to paving roads to fighting. But in the early years of the Section, there was skepticism among some intelligence officers about the possibility that Jews could really pass as Arabs and spy effectively. The old method of paying collaborators was proven, and what Sama'an was building may have seemed like a fantasy.

But after hostilities began in 1948, the Section proved to be one of the only effective intelligence tools the Jews had. The early intelligence services were mostly inadequate, the historians Benny Morris and Ian Black have written; Jewish leaders had little idea what the Arab side was thinking, and decisions were made in the dark. The Arab Section was a singular exception, according to Morris and Black, an outfit that "brought back useful information about Arab morale and military preparedness." This is what Dror, the author of the Section's official history, meant when he wrote decades later that "the nucleus of the way we conduct espionage begins with 'The Dawn.'" If Arab spies were needed, the Jews wouldn't pay them—they would be them. The Section came up with its own way of working: "We didn't learn it from anyone, from any teacher or school. We were the school," one of them recalled. "We improvised, saw what worked, and used it." Israel's intelligence doctrine, the agent said, was built "on our backs."

It was a curious feature of life in the Arab Section that the men refused to call themselves agents or spies, as I've been doing in these pages. Those terms were considered dishonorable. Instead they chose a peculiar word, one that exists in Hebrew and Arabic but has no parallel in English. The word, *mista'arvim* in Hebrew, or *musta'aribin* in Arabic, translates as "ones who become like Arabs." The name was an old one. It was used in Isaac's community of Aleppo, for example, to mean the native Jews who'd always been in the city and who adopted Arab culture after the Islamic conquest of 637 CE. The name differentiated them from the second part of the community, the *sepharadim*, who'd arrived only after the Spanish expulsion of 1492. This strange name, *mista'arvim*, is an important one in our story, and I don't want to lose its meaning. So despite the length and inelegance I'm going to translate it literally: Ones Who Become Like Arabs.

Today the shorthand for Jews from the Islamic world is Mizrahim, or "easterners," while Jews from the Christian world are known as Ashkenazim, from an old Hebrew word for Germany. Both terms are gross oversimplifications but occasionally unavoidable. The teacher was looking for Mizrahim. The ideal agent, the teacher Sam'an wrote, "must first of all be the son of an eastern Jewish community, native to one of the neighboring Arab countries or North Africa, his language and mother tongue Arabic, who had contact with his Arab neighbors in his home country or lived near them."

That meant his pool of potential Ones Who Become Like Arabs was small to begin with: in the 1940s, nine of every ten Jews in Palestine came from Europe.

Another difficulty was that Sam'an could offer no reward. It wasn't just that the Palmach couldn't pay salaries. The unit couldn't always cover bus fare or a cheap plate of hummus for lunch, and on at least one occasion agents had to stop trailing a target because they didn't have money for a night in a hostel. The fighters sometimes called the Palmach the barefoot army. It ran on ingenuity and willpower, on *the idea*. The Section needed men idealistic enough to risk their lives for free, but deceitful enough to make good spies. There weren't many who matched that description. Most of the candidates who showed up didn't last.

Sam'an was interested not just in the high Islam of theology, which you could read about in books, but in the everyday religion of ordinary people. Anyone could learn the Five Pillars: bearing witness that Muhammad is God's prophet; prayer; charity; the Ramadan fast; the hajj to Mecca. But how were you to place your hands on your body when praying? What Quran verses might pepper daily conversation? How could you become like an Arab to such an extent that you would be taken for an Arab by an Arab?

The recruits were from the Islamic world, but at home they'd known little of the majority religion beyond the danger it posed to people like them. Now they learned laws, scripture, superstitions, and figures of speech. Because they'd been affected by their time among the Ashkenazi pioneers, they also had to be taught manners. "The *sabras* are notorious for their complete disregard of form and formality," the Middle East scholar S. D. Goitein wrote with regret in the 1950s, referring to the culture gap between his fellow Israelis and their Arab neighbors. "Good manners and politeness are suspect. On the other hand, the whole social life of the Arabs is dominated by a carefully observed etiquette. An Arab would address you politely, even if he wished you to go to hell, while the young men of Israel are sometimes rude, even where they have every reason to be polite." If the recruits were to pass for Arabs, this would have to be fixed.

They memorized the opening verse of the Quran—the one that begins *In the name of Allah, the Compassionate and Merciful*—and some of the shorter chapters. They learned about the Prophet's night journey to Jerusalem astride a mystic beast named al-Buraq, and his meetings in a cave in the Arabian desert with the angel Jibril, the Arabic name for Gabriel. A few years later, after the founding of the State of Israel and its intelligence arms, all of this would be codified and organized into courses taught by professionals, but Sam'an was creating the course as he went along. It all added up to a new and idiosyncratic body of knowledge that they called, in Hebrew, *torat ha-hista'arvut*. That can be translated correctly as "the doctrine of Arab cover," or as "the Torah of becoming like an Arab."

From camp they set out to practice in Arab markets, sitting in barbershops and restaurants. They struck up conversations on buses. Mixed cities like Jerusalem and Haifa were good places to practice, because if you were exposed you might escape to a Jewish neighborhood or a British police station. The different dialects of Arabic, which give away a speaker's sect, class, and region, were one pitfall. You might be a One Who Becomes Like an Arab, but like what kind of Arab? Peasant? Worker? From Galilee, Nablus, or Bethlehem? You had to remember that if you didn't want something, in Syrian dialect you'd say *ma biddi*, but here in Palestine you said *biddish*. You had to remember the names of spices, tools, and cuts of meat in butcher's shops, all of which varied from place to place.

Many Jews in Palestine believed they spoke Arabic. They didn't. Many believed they knew Arab culture. They didn't. The ideal candidate, in the teacher's words, "isn't just a young man with dark skin and a mustache who knows how to speak Arabic, who shows up in an Arab area, drinks coffee, stays for a moment or two, and goes on his way." Succeeding, he wrote,

> means appearing as an Arab in every aspect: the way you look, talk, and behave, where you live, and where you enjoy yourself, including the right cover, papers, life story, and background. You must be a talented actor playing the part twenty-four hours a day, a role that comes at a cost of constant mental tension, and which is nerve-wracking to the point of insanity.

Something complicated was happening in that tent, and it's still hard to untangle exactly what it was. Who were these men? They were certainly not Muslims, which is why they had to learn Islam. But were they Arabs? They would have said no, and most Arabs would have said no. But they were native to the Arab world—as native as Arabs. If the key to belonging to the Arab nation was the Arabic language, as the Arab nationalists claimed, they were inside. So were they really "becoming like Arabs"? Or were they already Arabs? Were they pretending to be Arabs, or were they pretending to be people who weren't Arabs pretending to be Arabs?

Isaac and most of the others had run away from their fate in the Arab world to join the pioneers who'd come from Europe to build a new Jewish future. And here they were, worry beads in their hands, and their forehead on the mat. They were being offered entrance into the inner sanctum of this compelling society, a chance not available to most people like them. But there was a unique price: they had to become the people they'd fled.

It's impossible to conclude a description of the Arab Section in the period of preparation before the war without mentioning the famous bonfires. Havakuk played the flute at these evenings, and so did Ezra, the one who used to practice torturing himself and who was destined to be tortured for real. Isaac did some of the singing, his glasses gleaming in the firelight. Some of the songs would start slow, and then the drums fashioned from big olive tins picked up the rhythm, and a circle formed around the fire, each man's arm on the shoulder next to him. One memorable description has "the bespectacled Isaac Shoshan, a rope in his hand, making Menashkeh Abayov dance wearing a sack and a tail, like a monkey." An important ceremonial feature was coffee: You held the little tin pot with the long handle, the *finjan*, over the flame until the water boiled, and repeated this exactly seven times, allowing the liquid to calm each time. Only then was it ready to serve.

All kinds of people used to show up. The fighters of the regular Palmach, nearly all of them of eastern European origin, had an innocent admiration for the Arabs of their imagination, noble nomads, men of the soil. They peppered their Hebrew with Arabic and draped checked headscarves around their necks. They prized the Ones Who Become Like Arabs for their ability to go back and forth across the country's otherwise impassable human border, which seemed like a kind of magic. The campfires drew figures like Yitzhak Sadeh, the Palmach commander, and Yigal Allon, the officer and future general who was one of the Section's founders.

When the Section was camped outside Kibbutz Alonim, in Galilee, one of the visitors was a pretty fighter named Mira, who was seventeen. She appears in one photograph with curly hair, shorts, and the two most important features of Palmach photographs: a rifle and a confident grin.

Mira lived at Kibbutz Alonim, and still does. Back then, she wandered over to the campfire to see who the men were. They stood out, she remembered, because they were "black." Mira was born to Yemeni parents herself, so she fit in. She'd go over to the fire pit in the evenings and sing along. The flute player Havakuk, who was also Yemeni, caught her eye and she his, and that was how they found each other.

Many of the campfire numbers were in Arabic, love songs the guys remembered from home, with characters like the neighbor's beautiful daughter who becomes modern, leaves her father's house, and exchanges her modest *abaya* for a fashionable dress. Or one about old Hajj Muhammad and his horse, and another called "Jinantini" ("You've Driven Me Crazy"). Because the campfires were so popular in the Palmach, and because the Palmach was so central to the creation of Israeli society, the gatherings ended up acting as a portal through which pieces of the Arab world passed into the culture of the new Jewish state. An anthology of Palmach songs and stories compiled by two famous poets who served in those days includes a list of Arabic words that reached modern Hebrew via the fighters' slang: *halas, ya'ani, mabsut, mabruk, sahbak,* and dozens of others still in common use. The anthology includes the Arabic songs from the campfires, which the authors call "the songs of a neighbor people, a brother people, whom we didn't want to meet as an enemy." During my time as a soldier fifty years later we still brewed our coffee seven times.

The favorite campfire song was "From Beyond the River," sung in Hebrew to a melancholy tune of vaguely Middle Eastern character:

> From beyond the river we wandered here.
> We crossed desert sands, infinite and endless.
> With a tent, and great herds
> With a tent, and great herds;
> In a place of terrible heat,
> Where even at night the fire burns.

The ballad was distilled from the Arabian night by the poet Shaul Tchernichovsky of Mikhailovka, Russia. But it was a moving song, especially the way it was performed those nights. No one recorded it at the time, but a re-creation of the campfire version by an early entertainment troupe in the Israeli army preserves something of the original: a few voices repeat the phrase "Let's go forward, only forward," establishing the contemplative rhythm of the song, before other voices come in with the verse, and it gets faster and faster until everyone's on their feet and ecstatic. Jewish kids from Arab cities singing a song of desert nomads by a Russian—it captures the weird power of those times. The Jews of the 1940s didn't have herds, but they'd crossed perilous expanses to get here, and fires of their own.

In the State of Israel years later, when Mizrahi Jews began developing a political consciousness critical of the state's Ashkenazi founders and the official mythologies, a different memory surfaced. Yehuda Nini served in a Hagana platoon of Yemeni kids decimated in the Independence War: "There are units that tell how many they lost—this one told how many survived," he wrote in an important 1971 essay. The essay wasn't actually about the war. Nini was trying to make a point about the neglect of Mizrahi Jews by the state, the way they were being pushed to the periphery of Israeli society. He opened by returning to the nights when his platoon had campfires with coffee and spirited Arabic songs, like those of the Arab Section, also attended by Ashkenazi spectators from other units. "I felt the insult after a campfire that ended at dawn—" he wrote,

> The insult that they liked to come and watch us in our happiness, listen to our songs, eat our bread, drink from the strong, aromatic coffee that we made according to the ancient rules—boil seven times, subside seven times, and

one tap against the devil, may God curse him. They would come with their girls as if coming to see a circus; they wouldn't soil their hands with soot or let their eyes tear up with smoke, and our blankets would be given to them and their girls to pad their seats. They finished eating and disappeared into the darkness. The show was over.

If anyone from the Arab Section felt the same, I found no record of it. The atmosphere in the Palmach elite may have been different than in regular units like the one in the essay. Or perhaps the spies' lives in Israel afterward gave them fewer reasons to look back in anger. In retrospect, we understand that our men had found their way into one of the only corners of the Zionist movement where their identity was valued. A sole note of cynicism can be found in Gamliel's oral recollections, where he describes the bonfires as a kind of performance for the commanders who controlled the Palmach budget. "They'd come, and we'd dress like Arabs to impress the great men because we needed money to continue our missions," he remembered. "Sometimes we'd buy a little sheep and build a bonfire, we'd sing songs in Arabic and Hebrew, and then we'd slaughter the sheep." Gamliel hated killing, and his heart went out to the sheep: "Even in a celebration, you see, someone has to be the victim."

For the most part, though, the spies remembered these evenings with something close to rapture. "Sometimes I thought that more than our bonfire gave off sparks every night, we were all giving off sparks," one wrote, "sparks that came from the incredible reservoir of strength and preparedness in which we lived."

It was from this unusual little world that Gamliel the intellectual emerged in January 1948 on his way to his mission in Beirut, and from which Isaac the janitor's son emerged into Arab Haifa the following month with a bag of sunflower seeds and orders to tail the Muslim preacher known as Nimr, the one marked for death by Operation Starling.

The image of Isaac on those streets evokes a character dreamed up a few years earlier by two other Jewish kids in distant Cleveland, Ohio. Like Clark Kent, Isaac attracted no attention from the people he passed. He seemed like another poor worker, one of thousands. But he wasn't what they thought. He wasn't his previous self, or his father or grandfather, cowering in their shadow. He had a secret power.

7: Operation Starling

When the target left his home on one of the streets near the port each morning, Isaac / Abdul Karim was sitting on the curb, his gaze averted, keeping Nimr in the corner of his eye. He cracked seeds between his teeth, tasted the salt, and spat the shells at his feet. When the cleric, in his robes and conical hat, crossed among the donkey carts and hustlers in Hamra Square with his bodyguards, Isaac observed them from the far side of the plaza. The preacher owned a shop that sold Islamic literature, and Isaac kept an eye on the storefront, memorizing Nimr's movements to and from work, paying special attention if a customer stood out as someone not really buying books.

The first plan was to send two pairs of assassins across the urban seam line on foot. They'd wait outside Nimr's home, shoot him at short range, and escape back across the line in a taxi driven by another agent. But on the day of the operation, illness put one of the first pairs out of action. The second pair went in anyway, but when they lurked for forty-five minutes with no sign of the target, the neighbors became suspicious and they had to leave.

The next day they tried again, leaving thirty-six minutes later.

Trying the same plan a third time was too risky, so a new idea was hatched: a sniper would shoot Nimr from a fortified Jewish post in a house bordering the Arab sector. If the source of the shot was identified, however, the British army was likely to punish the

Jewish forces by destroying the post; the soldiers of the British garrison ventured out of their bases less and less as the pullout approached, but they still intervened when one side went too far. The fortified position would be vital when the final battle for Haifa came, so it wasn't worth it, and the planners dropped the idea. As these discussions continued, Isaac realized that the target was gone. Unaware that his demise had been close on two occasions or that details of the third were being decided, the preacher had gone to Damascus to lobby the Syrian government for guns.

A Jewish spy at the Haifa telephone exchange discovered the date of his return and the route—the highway down the coast from Lebanon. A new plan was drawn up. Two cars would await him at a traffic circle north of Haifa, where Nimr's driver would have to slow down. The first car would carry the hit team, and the second would have an Arab Section spotter to identify Nimr. The spotter was Isaac. That's how two people who were born not far from each other and who spoke the same language—one a Muslim cleric and the other a kid from the Jewish Quarter—collided on a road in Palestine as their histories traveled in opposite directions.

The act of violence that followed is documented by the participants themselves from different angles, and with remarkably few discrepancies. That being the case, it's best to let them tell it themselves:

> ISAAC: We set out early in the morning to the ambush spot. I sat in the car and looked at every car reaching the traffic circle from the north. I had no information telling me what kind the sheikh would be driving. . . . There was also a possibility that the sheikh would disguise

himself to avoid being recognized, and I needed to be completely sure it was him. Any mistake could mean the death of innocents.

After a few hours of watching cars enter the traffic circle, my vision was blurring. Sometimes I thought I saw the sheikh, but I wasn't sure. Too many people looked like him. I felt my nerves slacken.

NIMR: The car took us forward, covering ground swiftly. We left Acre behind us, and lo and behold, here was Haifa. How beautiful you are, Haifa, bride of the East, jewel of the world! You have the mountain, the valley, and the plain, the sea beneath your feet, the river by your side. You are woven into all of this as the stars are woven into the sky.

ISAAC: Just as doubt crept into my heart and I began to fear the sheikh had slipped by, a car appeared with five people inside. A single glance was enough: one of them was the sheikh. The many hours I'd spent following him in the previous months made him more familiar to me than I'd realized. I could recognize him by his steps, by the angle of his head, by his beard.

PALMACH REPORT: At ten o'clock the car passed, and the spotter saw Nimr inside. Our two cars set out immediately in pursuit. The traffic on the road was heavy, and two British army convoys coming from different directions made it hard to catch up with Nimr's car. The spotter's car managed to pass it and slow it down, and also to signal to the first car that this was the target.

ISAAC: I gave them the signal—a handkerchief held out the car window, as if to dry it in the wind.

NIMR: As the car jumped along I looked at Haifa—sometimes at its mountain opposite me, sometimes at its green valleys next to me. . . . This is truly the land of happiness, the place of basil and the sleepy narcissus.

And as I dream, wide awake, of these views, suddenly a traitorous car of Jews passes us with lightning speed—

ISAAC: We passed, slowed down, and forced the sheikh's car to do the same. In the mirror we could see the assassination team's car appear quickly and draw alongside the sheikh's car, driving in the left lane. We saw the barrels of the tommy guns poking out of the windows—

NIMR: —before it had passed our car they had fired almost a thousand bullets from the fast-shooting machine guns they carried. Lead fell upon us like the patter of rain.

MALINKI, GUNMAN IN THE FIRST CAR: We fired bursts at the vehicle, we hit it, and it swerved. We raced ahead.

NIMR: O Allah the Good! I uttered an anguished cry without meaning to—O the Good, the Protector! And so the Good was revealed in his goodness, and the Protector in his protection and grace.

Our car came to a halt, as it was shot to pieces, the fragments of its windows scattered by the bullets. I looked behind me. Blood spurted from the head of our comrade el-Majdoub as if he were a burbling spring, because of a bullet that punctured his skull. May Allah's mercy be upon him. I looked at the driver, Muhsen, and blood streamed from his head, face, and chest. And I looked at myself and saw blood coming from my left shoulder and dripping from my right hand . . .

My right hand crippled, unmoving . . .

I gave the door a strong push, took my pistol from my pocket, and began to fall to the ground. The driver shouted, "What do you want, sir?"

I said, "I want to fight back."

He said, "Sir! They shot and got away. Should I drive quickly, and then we might escape?"

I said, "Can you?"

He said, "I'll try." . . .

The car began to move, but very slowly. I looked ahead and back and saw no one coming or going. The road was empty, and this is a road where the movement of cars never stops even for a minute or a second. I understood that this was a well-laid plan, this ruse of theirs. The car continued to drive with the dead man behind us soaking in his blood—how sweet is his soul, as they say. He was making wounded sounds of rasping and whistling.

The car drove until it came to the intersection where there's a traffic circle linking three roads—the Balad el-Sheikh road, the Acre-Beirut road, and the Haifa road. I stole a quick glance outside, and here were the criminal Jews standing guard on the other side of the circle, the side leading to Balad el-Sheikh. I saw one of them raise his head in the window of the car.

ISAAC: I wanted to get out with the pistol and perform what today they would call "confirming the kill." But the others said no, it's enough.

NIMR: I don't know what prevented them from killing us, with no one else on the road to see, and what stopped them from shooting us when they were no more than a few meters away!

It was the watchfulness of Allah, who didn't leave us for a moment. Our car continued to drive slowly, and the driver said, "I'm finished, I have no blood left." I encouraged him, saying, "Here, Haifa is just a few meters away. We've reached the gates of the city." . . . And he was truly brave, and didn't yield, and was patient and unafraid, and didn't lose his nerve or judgment. As for me—I had no doubt that I was dead. I saw my blood flowing. I believed that bullets had entered my body and that breath would remain in my corpse for only a few more minutes or hours.

The car kept going, with me encouraging the driver, and praising his fortitude, and expressing my desire to reach our destination, until he nearly lost consciousness and could drive no more.

PALMACH REPORT: The car with the spotter, which had stayed behind to see what happened, caught up with the first car, and when they told the first team that Nimr's car continued toward Haifa, the men of the first car deployed along the road to attack it again. But they didn't recognize the car. Only after it passed did they spot it, and Nimr himself, and begin to give pursuit, but it managed to get into the populated Arab area. Our men returned to base without attacking a second time.

NIMR: We had already reached Nazareth Street, the first street in Haifa, and I saw a few Arabs and motioned to them. They rushed over. When they saw the car with its shattered windshield and perforated metal, they understood what the criminal Jews had done.

The young men began to shout, and gathered around from all directions. They raced me to another car. I told them to care for the driver and for the martyr.

THE ARABIC DAILY *EL-DIFAA*, THE NEXT MORNING:
HIS HONOR SHEIKH MUHAMMAD NIMR EL-KHATIB
WOUNDED IN TRAITOROUS ATTACK
Mr. Omar el-Majdoub was fatally wounded, and Mr. Muhammad Muhsen Fakhr el-Din was lightly wounded. The sheikh was hit by three bullets in the shoulder, and his life is not in danger. The wounded were transferred immediately to El-Amin Hospital for emergency care, and his honor Sheikh Muhammad Nimr was taken to Government Hospital.

NIMR: I don't know what happened next. I awoke to the sound of crowds who came to find out what the news meant. I saw nothing but the tears of loyalty, I felt nothing but the kisses of brotherhood, and from every direction I heard the voices of prayer.... Some of the Brothers came to me, bloodstained and armed. They upheld their oath and never flagged in their quest for vengeance.

8: Cedar

The wounded preacher was spirited out of Palestine to safety in Beirut, but his war was over and the battle for Haifa would be decided without him. He never went home. For a time, he unknowingly shared the Lebanese capital with another new arrival from Palestine, Yussef el-Hamed, who'd also been displaced by the fighting, or so he said.

The latter was a man of twenty-five. He had no family with him but did seem to have some means, the sum of which sufficed to open a women's clothing shop by the Cinema Salwa, and the source of which wouldn't have borne scrutiny should anyone have thought to check. Gamliel/Yussef's instructions had been to settle in and wait. That was all. Events were moving so fast when he left Palestine that it was impossible to get more specific. Afterward more agents might arrive, if the Jews held out. They said it could be months, which was absurd—the pace of developments in 1948 was measured in hours, not months. It wasn't clear who would come, if anyone, and when that would be, if ever.

While operating inside Palestine, the men of the Arab Section knew that if they came under suspicion they could try to escape back across the line to a Jewish area, or throw themselves on the mercy of the British police. The Jewish leadership could try to intervene, or the Palmach could try to spring them. None of this applied in the heart of Lebanon. Here no one could help Gamliel, and the danger was driven home with some regularity. On a bus one day, for example, he heard shouting and watched as a few men dragged another passenger off into the street. The passenger looked strange, they said, and spoke broken Arabic. They suspected him of being a Jewish spy, but after a few minutes it turned out he was just a Lebanese immigrant to South America who'd come back to see his homeland. They let him go. A talkative man sitting next to Gamliel/Yussef then turned to him and, after offering him a banana and questioning him about his background, suggested that perhaps he was a Zionist himself. There was an aspect of Gamliel's presentation that seems to have drawn the attention of some of the people he met; he doesn't seem to have known what it was, so neither do we. Gamliel denied the charge, of course. But it was unsettling, another lesson about how close he was to the edge.

In their own descriptions of the time, the men don't make much of their own heroism, and seem to take their actions for granted. It would be a mistake for us to do the same. When you're a soldier, you have hierarchy and protocol, and comrades who surround you and cushion the blows. Gamliel was a kind of soldier, but he had no officers or uniform. His comrades were too far away to matter. That's the way it is for spies. But if you're spying for the CIA, you have Langley and the United States of America. You might not see them from your street corner or hotel room, but you know they exist, and their power is a comfort. These men had no such thing. They had no country—in early 1948, Israel was a wish, not a fact. If they disappeared, they'd be gone. No one might find them. No one might even look. The future was blank. And still they set out into those treacherous times, alone.

Because Gamliel was in Lebanon he was given the code name Cedar, in keeping with the Jews' occasional practice of using code names vulnerable to third graders of average intelligence. Agents running clandestine immigration from Iraq at this time, for example, used the code name *artzi* to mean the Land of Israel; the word means "my land." And for a while one member of the Hagana command, a Frenchman, had the code name Frenchman. But in the early months of 1948 it wasn't very important what Gamliel's code name was, because he had no way to communicate at all.

Gamliel's store was at Ouzai, now a concrete slum by Beirut's international airport, but then a sleepy area by a lovely beach, removed from the noise of the city center. That stretch of coast would turn out to be lightly trafficked at night, which was lucky, and to have sand soft enough for the rapid burial of whatever one might need to rapidly bury. Less fortuitous than the location was Gamliel's choice of merchandise; women's clothing didn't seem to be in demand, at least not the kind he was selling, leaving the shop empty most of the time. This was a problem not only because Gamliel needed the money but because remaining open without customers might raise questions about his income. He began selling sweets instead.

He listened for information that he thought could be useful, and tried to grasp the landscape of the city and its people, but had no way to pass anything on. Most of his recollections of those months are about learning the candy business—how much he paid for a kilo of sugar, where he bought equipment, a business contact who was Shiite, another who was Druze. He had a few uncomfortable conversations, like one with the owner of a little grocery store nearby who seems to have had sharp senses. You know what? said this man one day, in Gamliel's recollection. So far we haven't heard you say a word about your family. Not a word.

This was an innocent question, and also a gun at Gamliel's temple. He knew this feeling by now.

I'm miserable inside—what can I say about them? responded Gamliel, employing the Arab Section's usual tactic with regard to family members. All I can tell you is that my whole family was killed, that no one is left, that I myself barely escaped and am barely getting by. I have nothing else to say.

That seemed to work, and the man left him alone. There were many people in Beirut with stories like that.

It made sense that Gamliel was the first agent sent abroad, the scout. He could pull off middle-class cover, unlike the others, who tended to play workers, and before the war he seems to have been the one sent when a mission required good language skills and heightened political awareness. It was Gamliel who wrote many of the Section's best intelligence reports up to that point: on the Muslim Brotherhood rally where he'd seen Nimr; on a temperate gathering of Arab Communists, whose leader had just returned from meeting comrades in London; on a rowdy nationalist gathering where money was raised for the war against the Jews. His political sensitivities, however, were directed not only at the opposing side but at his own.

Gamliel reached Palestine in the middle of the Second World War, running away from the Jewish Quarter of Damascus and sneaking across the border. There was no future for him as a Jew among Arabs, that was clear, and he wanted to join the Zionists and become a pioneer. Where he grew up, you always knew you were supposed to return to the Land of Israel eventually. The Jews prayed thrice daily, "May our eyes see thy return to Zion in mercy," and during the festive Passover Seders of his childhood, Gamliel remembers each participant in the traditional meal taking a piece of unleavened bread on one shoulder, as if they were carrying a great weight, like a slave of Pharaoh. The others would ask, in Arabic, "Where do you come from?"

"Egypt."

"And where are you going?"

"Jerusalem."

Then everyone around the table said, "Inshallah," if Allah wills it, because when the Jews spoke Arabic they called God by his Arabic name, like everyone else. In the astonishing circumstances of the mid-twentieth century, God suddenly willed it, and by 1944 Gamliel was on a kibbutz in the Land of Israel, doing his best to be a reborn Hebrew of the kind imagined by the Zionist movement, a farmer and a fighter, free of Diaspora shackles.

But he discovered quickly that he wasn't like the other young people on Kibbutz Ein Harod. He spoke like an Arab and looked like an Arab, and the sabras thought he was strange. He began using his Hebrew name, Gamliel, instead of the Arabic name of his childhood, Jamil, but that didn't solve the problem. His music was Oum Kalthoum, the great Egyptian chanteuse, and the oud genius Abd el-Wahab, but here the only records were European symphonies. The food was bland, with none of the familiar spices. Once, he asked the woman who ran the communal kitchen for some oil so he could cook a Middle Eastern dish for himself and a few other young Syrians, and she said no, they had to eat in the communal dining hall with everyone else. Did they think they were different?

Sometimes he and the other Syrian boys would spend their evenings apart, speaking Arabic by themselves, but he hadn't come to the Land of Israel for that. He made Ashkenazi friends and sat with them as they talked about childhood friends or pretty girls they knew. But he couldn't talk about his old life in Damascus—they weren't interested. "Because I was the one who wanted to join them, and not the other way around," he remembered, "I was the one who was worn down, who had to round his edges to fit the machine that spins around, sparing no one." This ability would prove useful later on. As a spy, Gamliel observed, "You need the instinct of a person who knows how to fit in, to remove the sharp angles and curve into the society." But when he wasn't a spy yet, just a proud youth perceptive enough to notice condescension, it hurt to round his edges.

Then the Arab Section spotted him precisely because of the difference he was trying to escape. Gamliel couldn't turn down a call to serve the nation in the Palmach, so from the kibbutz he went to the Section camp and found that he'd gone back, in his description, "to the way things were, to the society of Arabs, of easterners," which was exactly what he'd wanted to leave behind.

Palmach platoons were housed on kibbutzim, but it took an unusually long time to find one willing to take in this particular unit, and in the years before the war the men were shuffled from place to place. The reason usually given for the lack of hospitality was the absence of women in the Section, which made it exceptional among the egalitarian units of the Palmach. Most Jewish parents from the Arab world hadn't jettisoned traditional mores, and thought it dishonorable for unmarried daughters to go off with strange men. Without women fighters, the Section couldn't help with jobs that women tended to do in the kibbutz kitchens and children's houses, and that made the unit less useful to the hosts, who were giving the fighters room and board in return for labor.

That, at least, was the official explanation. Gamliel didn't believe it. "They were worried, there were all kinds of concerns, and it was mainly because we were from the communities of the East," he wrote afterward. "Communities of the East" meant Jews from the Islamic world. At one kibbutz, he remembered, the Section's men were actually building their tents when the members voted that they couldn't stay. He never forgot the insult. Some of the other men remembered that members of a few kibbutzim warned their daughters to stay clear of the "blacks" from the Section. The warnings seem to have been only partially successful, but they stung.

Particularly bitter for Gamliel was the time two groups of orphaned refugee children arrived at one kibbutz where the Section camped for a time. The first group was from Europe, the second from Syria. The kibbutz held an assembly to distribute the children among adopted families, and hands went up for the Ashkenazi kids but none for the Syrians. The members started to explain: Maybe we don't know their mentality, maybe they don't know what discipline is yet and don't know how to get by in a family. After Gamliel listened to it all, he wrote a furious article for the kibbutz newsletter comparing the members to Nazis. When he refused to tone it down, the article wasn't published. In the end all the kids were taken in, but it still bothered him.

He never doubted the cause, though, then or afterward. He knew the Jews needed their own state, and knew better than the arrivals from Europe what they'd have to face to get one. He never stopped feeling the pull of the pioneers' world. One of his most powerful memories from the months before he left for Beirut is of a trip he took while on a short leave from the unit, a visit with friends who were building a new kibbutz under the vast skies of the Negev Desert. They were living simply, speaking Hebrew, raising a community from nothing—the Zionist dream, Gamliel's own dream when he first came to the Land, before his story became more complicated.

He joined them on a walk from their huts to a nearby field to check the progress of some wheat they'd planted. It had sprouted!

Nothing could have made them happier. It was all they wanted, for a plot of barren land to turn green. Land was land. Rain was rain. Wheat was wheat.

He didn't know it at the time, but Gamliel of the Arab Section—previously the child Jamil Cohen of the Jewish Quarter of Damascus, also the Muslim shopkeeper Yussef el-Hamed of Beirut—had long years of false identity ahead of him. His cover as an Israeli agent would be so deep one day that his marriage would have to be conducted in a secret Jewish ceremony somewhere in Europe. One of his daughters would spend the first years of her life with an Arabic name, Samira, reverting to her Hebrew name, Mira, only when the mission ended. That's beyond the scope of this book, but things were never going to be simple. It was never going to be wheat and rain.

His closest friend from the kibbutz group, a young woman named Batsheva, understood the way he was torn and sent a book to keep his spirits up. It was about Hannah Senesh, a poet from Hungary who came to the Land and then volunteered to be dropped back behind Axis lines in 1944. She was twenty-three when she was captured, tortured, and shot. Batsheva had inscribed the front:

> Gamliel—
> When faced with the grim moment of the test, will each of us know to stand in the place chosen for us by fate?

He didn't want to be like an Arab anymore. But when the young poet leapt into the sky over occupied Europe, she'd known the place chosen for her by fate. So would he.

. . .

AFTER GAMLIEL'S RETURN to Beirut in the middle of February, the war in Palestine only got worse. The British, counting the days until the end of the Mandate, could no longer control the combatants. The armies of the Arab states would invade as soon as the British were gone. "The balance of the fighting," observed the British High Commissioner, "seems to have turned much in favor of the Arabs." There were Jewish successes like the removal of the preacher, but that wasn't even a decisive blow in the battle for Haifa, let alone in the war. The relief of Jerusalem was failing under attack from the Holy Jihad force and its skilled commander, Abd el-Qader el-Husseini. The city's Jews were beginning to starve. While Gamliel was out of contact in Beirut, one of his friends, Poza, died in a Jewish rout at Nebi Samwil with a few dozen other fighters. But Gamliel found out only long afterward.

He did his best to play the part of a Palestinian Arab patriot. In April, word came of one of the first major reversals suffered by the Arab side—not a battle, exactly, but a case of mistaken identity. It concerned the Holy Jihad commander el-Husseini, who was fighting Jewish forces for the village of Qastel along the Jerusalem road. At dawn one foggy morning the Arab commander took two of his men and climbed up toward the battle line, where a Jewish sentry mistook them for Jews and hailed them. "Hello, boys," he called out—but in Arabic, *marhaba ya jama'a*, not because he thought the figures were Arabs but because the Jewish fighters liked using Arabic words among themselves.

The Arab commander doesn't seem to have understood exactly where he was, and responded, oddly, in English: "Hello, boys!" He might have thought the soldiers were some of the British deserters serving under his command. The Jewish sentry realized his error first and opened fire, killing the officer who'd spoken English, who turned out to be the Arab commander himself. El-Husseini's enraged fighters then captured the village, killing the Arabic-speaking Jewish sentry, but abandoned it the next day to attend their commander's funeral, allowing the Hagana to regain control. The village was later repopulated with Jews from Kurdistan. The death of the great el-Husseini seemed to demand a response from his countryman Yussef el-Hamed, so the spy hung a poster of the martyr in the window of his shop.

But for the most part the war was felt only faintly in Beirut. Gamliel watched and listened and tried not to slip. He "curved" into his new life, as he knew how to do, and found that his Arab identity was less an act as time went on. He felt himself adopting the personality of the people around him, seeing things their way. Others have found the same, in life and literature. In describing the double game of Alec Leamas in East Germany in *The Spy Who Came In from the Cold*, John le Carré reminds us that Balzac is said to have asked on his deathbed about the well-being of his fictional characters. "Similarly Leamas, without relinquishing the power of invention, identified himself with what he had invented," writes le Carré. "Only very rarely, as now, going to bed that evening, did he allow himself the dangerous luxury of admitting the great lie he lived."

9: The Watcher (2)

A small canister slipped into a metal tube somewhere on the slopes of Mount Carmel, at a point overlooking the Arab streets huddled by the Haifa harbor. With a pop it shot back out, ascending into a dawn sky that was pale pink and orange on the eastern horizon. At the top of its arc gravity reasserted itself, and the cylinder paused over the stricken city and the steely surface of the bay. Then it plunged toward the warehouses of the port, the Ottoman clock tower, red-shingled roofs, cypress boughs, and limestone walls, finally striking asphalt in front of Ibrahim, the Arab port worker whom we last met looking around a militia building, and who'd watched the *Exodus* arrive with his comrades on a hull-cleaning crew. When the shell landed, Ibrahim saw the explosion lift another man and dash him against a wall.

It was April 22, 1948, two weeks after the death of el-Husseini, two months after the bomb in the garage and the attempted assassination of the preacher—the decisive day for Haifa, and a bad day to be here. The Jews up on Mount Carmel sent more shells after the first, and Ibrahim ran back in the direction of the El-Nil flophouse, where he shared a room with a few other workers. We know what happened to him because he wrote it all down in detail immediately afterward.

The shelling didn't catch him completely by surprise; the previous day had been an alarming one. He'd been passing one of the Jewish posts fortified with cinder blocks and barrels when he heard the crack of a gunshot and dove for cover, and when he took off his cap he saw a neat bullet hole. He preserved the cap for the rest of his life as proof of divine providence. Providence proved limited, though, and the rest of his life was short.

At night, crowded around a radio with other guests back at the hostel, he'd heard a warning in Arabic from the Jewish propaganda station: The Arabs of Haifa should evacuate women, children, and the elderly. The listeners laughed at this empty threat. The Arabs were armed and ready to fight. What did the Jews think was about to happen? At midnight Ibrahim woke up to a barrage streaking down from Mount Carmel and pounding the Arab quarters in the lower city. He stayed awake for a while watching the fire and smoke rising from the eastern outskirts, near the Rushmiyeh Bridge. No one knew what was going on, but now no one laughed. He managed a few more hours of sleep and then set out into the streets again before sunrise, and that was when the shell barely missed him.

Other people ran by as the sky grew lighter. They were saying the Jews had captured Hamra Square in the heart of Arab Haifa and were still advancing. The day before, the violence seemed like just another raid or retaliation, but this time was different. The British had abruptly removed their troops from most of Haifa ahead of schedule; the soldiers were tired of being caught between the warring sides and withdrew to the port compound, leaving the Jewish and Arab militias to decide the city's fate. Arab units quickly attacked several Jewish positions and were beaten back.

Then columns of Hagana fighters, maneuvering like a real army, advanced into the Arab sector from different directions, coming along the flatland by the water and down one of the outdoor flights of stairs from Mount Carmel into the lower city. Arab fighters resisted around the Najada building, the one where Ibrahim had seen the uniformed militiamen, and the fighters trapped a Jewish platoon inside, killing four, wounding ten, and holding up the advance. The Arab National Council had put up posters exhorting people not to leave or lose hope:

> To the fighting nation:
> The National Council of Haifa informs you of first tidings:
> The plan to divide your country and tear off part of your
> homeland has failed. The dream of the enemy to establish
> a state on your ruins has been undone. . . . Long live
> Palestine—Arab, Independent, Free and United!

But by 10:00 a.m. there was chaos in the streets downtown. "Refugees fleeing the path of the advancing columns converged on the Old Town," as one Palestinian historian described the scene, "children in pajamas, men in old-fashioned nightshirts and undergarments, women carrying babies and bundles of household effects."

Instead of returning directly to the flophouse after he was caught in the shelling, Ibrahim stopped at a restaurant full of men speaking nervous Arabic. No one seemed to know what else to do. They could all hear the gunfire and explosions getting closer. New people burst into the restaurant every so often and were immediately surrounded and interrogated: What had they seen? Where were the Jews?

A man came from the street with a stirring declaration: "Rejoice, O Arabs, the Arab Legion has surrounded the Jews from the mountain and is cutting them down from above!" The Arab Legion was the army of Transjordan, commanded and supplied by the British, the best the Arab world had, so this was good news.

But if the man expected jubilation, he was disappointed. No one believed him. Soon someone else banged through the door and said the Arab Legion was nowhere to be seen.

Next a young man came in directly from the fighting. He was, Ibrahim saw, "armed, exhausted, and stunned." Someone rushed out a cup of coffee, and everyone urged him to talk. "I just came from Halisa among the last to get out," the fighter said, referring to one of the neighborhoods where the Jewish forces were advancing. "I was in a position with other men, and we showered them with fire and they answered with mortars. The screams of the women and children drove us crazy and we had to shut them up. Then a shell hit our position and we were forced to withdraw, and we ran until we reached you here."

What about the Arab Legion? someone asked. Weren't Arab forces coming to the aid of Haifa? The young fighter answered with "energetic curses" and vanished. Soon the restaurant's owner kicked everyone out, locked the door, and fled.

One of the street posters put up by the Arab leadership urged:

> Stay in your place. Reinforce your position.
> Repulse the attacks of the aggressor!

But now some of these same leaders ran away, including Haifa's military commander himself. Their men were soon in disarray, retreating past corpses in the street. The Jews had rigged a few vans with loudspeakers to accompany their ragged infantry, an attempt at psychological warfare, and residents heard distorted voices telling them in Arabic that the day of judgment had arrived. The Jews controlled all access to the city, the loudspeakers announced. No reinforcements were coming. Surrender.

After leaving the restaurant, Ibrahim found himself with a friend from Acre, an Arab town at the far tip of Haifa Bay. Ibrahim was known as a hard-liner, someone who opposed handing the Jews a victory by running away, and this friend from Acre was of the same mind. Too many had already run because of the bloodshed of recent months—first the workers who'd come to Haifa from elsewhere in the Arab world, who could simply return home, and the rich families who could afford to escape to relatives or summer residences, and then regular people who were too afraid to keep risking the daily violence. It was cowardly. But now the two of them decided to see how they could get away after all, if it came to that. British soldiers still held the port, and Acre, an hour away by boat, was safely in Arab hands. Everyone thought the Arab armies would soon arrive to defeat the Jews, so many saw logic in a temporary escape. It was with that contingency plan in mind that the two men cut through a grove of eucalyptus trees to the waterfront, and that was where Ibrahim glimpsed something he recorded as "sad and terrible"—an image that became the very symbol of the Palestinian tragedy later on, once the scale and permanence of the tragedy became clear.

Hundreds of people were mobbing the docks, trying to board the small boats leaving Haifa. The boats were ferrying refugees across the bay to Acre, but many hoped to get farther north, to Lebanon, far from the fighting and well behind Arab lines. Soon the number of people on the quays was in the thousands. The wounded preacher Nimr was in exile by then, but accounts from his hometown reached him, and his memoir describes the scene: "Men trampled each other, and women their own children. The boats at the port filled with live cargo. These boats had never seen such cargo."

There was shooting nearby as Jewish fighters pressed the assault in the lower city, and bullets wounded a few British marines guarding the gates to the port. Soon Jewish intelligence reported that no one was answering the phones at Arab headquarters. "The Arab hospitals are full of dead and wounded," the report said. "Corpses and wounded lie in the streets and are not collected for lack of organization and sanitary means; panic in the Arab street is great."

Neither Ibrahim nor anyone else understood the significance of what they were seeing. The British still ruled Palestine. There was no Jewish state. It was understood that the invasion of the Arab armies would begin within weeks, and though the Jews had shown surprising tenacity against Palestinian Arab irregulars, many doubted their chances against real soldiers. This mass exodus had seemed impossible even that morning. Haifa's Jewish mayor was at the port, begging people to stay, saying they wouldn't be harmed. The few who listened were not. But it was impossible to know that at the time. People heard stories of enemy atrocities, some of them true, and felt the impact of the shells. They feared for their lives.

The moment was immortalized in *Returning to Haifa*, a novella by the Palestinian writer Ghassan Kanafani. "The sky was on fire crackling with shots, bombs and explosions, near and far," he wrote. "It was as though the very sounds themselves were pushing everyone toward the port." A husband and wife meet amid the rush toward the waterfront:

> Around them passed the flood of humanity, pushing them from side to side, forcing them along toward the shore, but beyond that they were incapable of feeling anything

at all until they were splashed by spray flying up from the oars and they looked back toward shore to see Haifa clouding over behind the evening's dusk and the twilight of their tears.

Ibrahim watched it all unfold by the docks. The shops were closed, and the only food he could scrounge was a can of fruit, which he ate quickly in the street as people hurried past toward the water. He saw a confused old man sitting on some steps, sobbing. When Ibrahim asked if he could help, the man said his wife and six children were lost in the madness. The worker took him back to the El-Nil, where he discovered that the flophouse's owner had fled along with most of the guests.

The old man lay down on Ibrahim's cot, and when he calmed down he said his eldest son was with the militia fighting the Jews. He was worried to death about this son. Ibrahim tried to reassure him, saying he'd probably retreated with the other fighters. The man had no money, so Ibrahim gave him two pounds, and the old man fell asleep.

THE NEXT MORNING, Friday, the Arab streets of the lower city were deserted. The few people visible outside had expressions that were not just aggrieved but ashamed. It was impossible to grasp what had just happened. When Ibrahim found his friend from Acre packing to leave, the man felt the need to explain: Look at the effendis and the rich who already ran away, he said. Why should I stay? Ibrahim agreed that he was right and accompanied his friend into the street, where they finally encountered the enemy.

The Jews were men in khaki, knit caps, and an assortment of civilian shoes, with weapons manufactured in underground shops or left over from the world war. They were taking up positions around an intersection. One soldier pulled aside the man from Acre. Another turned his attention to Ibrahim, and if the man from Acre was paying attention he might have seen a curious interaction.

Come over here, buddy, the Jewish soldier said to Ibrahim. He spoke in a tone that wasn't hostile but surprised. And he spoke in Hebrew.

Then a thought seemed to occur to the soldier and his demeanor changed. *Ta'al hon, irfa idek*, he ordered in gruff Arabic. Come here, hands up.

Ibrahim did as he was told. If his friend from Acre was watching, he would have observed that Ibrahim was muttering something to the Jewish fighter who was patting him down. But we don't know what the man from Acre saw, because after the Jews let them both go, the man said good-bye to Ibrahim and they parted for good.

Ibrahim's freedom lasted for only a few minutes before he was stopped again on Stanton Street by another shout: *Waqef*. Halt. A new soldier was pointing a rifle at him and waving him over. The soldier searched his clothes before adding him to a crowd of Arab detainees sitting under guard nearby.

When Ibrahim joined the men squatting under the soldiers' guns, a few of the others told him they were waiting for a commander to decide what to do with them. After a while he was separated, led past at gunpoint, and ordered into the back of a truck.

PART II

Beirut

10: Kim

The creation of an agent who could convince you he was one of you—that had been the idea since the very beginning. The very beginning, for the Arab Section, was seven years before the fall of Haifa, in the spring of 1941, the darkest moment of the world war. The model was Kim. *Kim* isn't as popular as it once was, but among the Section's creators everyone knew the book and Kipling's Irish orphan, raised in the Lahore alleys, who could pass for Indian and became a British spy. There was something about costume and disguise, about one kind of person passing for another, that had a particular hold on the British imagination. Kim was an inspiration for many real-life spies, like the double agent Harold "Kim" Philby, who at the precise time of the Section's creation was in the early stages of his own complicated identity game as a Soviet mole inside Britain's secret service. Philby's father, St. John Philby, had himself "gone native" in Arabia, converting to Islam and taking the name Abdullah.

This was all part of the Arab Section's distinctive DNA, about which a few words will be useful before we follow our characters into the next stage of the Independence War. This book concerns a war between Jews and Arabs, but in fact the Arab Section wasn't created to fight Arabs at all. The original enemy was German. And the enterprise wasn't purely a Jewish one; rather it was an odd product of one of those brief relationships that make sense only in times of great excitement or terror. One chromosome came from the Palmach. The other came from the Mediterranean contingent of Britain's Special Operations Executive, people who ranged, in the words of the historian Antony Beevor, "from Philhellenic dons to well-connected thugs, with many variations in between including a handful of good regular soldiers, romantics, writers, scholar gypsies and the odd *louche* adventurer."

In 1941, with Europe lost, the Americans still sitting out the war, and the Afrika Korps advancing toward Egypt, it seemed likely that Palestine and the entire Middle East would soon be swallowed by the Third Reich. Things seemed so dire that Palestine's British rulers drew up plans for a last stand on Mount Carmel, like the Jewish zealots on Masada in the Roman wars. The maps still exist, with orderly circles marking the final defensive positions. What this would have meant for the Jews here was clear even before the precise details of their relatives' fate emerged from Europe.

Amid this panic, Zionist leaders set aside their anger with Britain for buckling to Arab pressure and reneging on the promise of a Jewish national home with the famous White Paper of 1939, and for turning away refugees trying to reach Palestine precisely when the need was most desperate. The Jews decided to cooperate and lobbied for a chance to fight. The established British authorities in Palestine didn't think it was a good idea to arm or train them, understanding that the same people would use what they'd learned from the British against the British as soon as the war was over. They were right. But the special operations officers who'd arrived in the region, who weren't part of the regular army, didn't care. They were concerned only with winning the war, not with colonial administration afterward. They saw the Jewish underground as something resembling the IRA, but they liked that.

You could work with it. They understood that no one was more committed to fighting the Nazis than the Jews, whom they called the Friends.

The Special Operations Executive opened a school outside Haifa to train spies and saboteurs to operate behind enemy lines— Jews, Greeks, Albanians, Yugoslavs, and others from around the Mediterranean. One of the trainers was the gifted travel writer Patrick Leigh Fermor, who later gained fame on Crete by kidnapping a German general. Another was Nicholas Hammond, remembered by the early Jewish recruits as their most steadfast ally, who'd been plucked from the Cambridge faculty because he knew Greek. ME 102, as the school was known, seems to have had a very literary staff. These were people, as the Israeli writer Yonatan Ben-Nahum noted in an essay on the origins of the Arab Section, who "all knew and quoted Kipling like the Bible." The figure of Kipling's Kim was familiar to the Jewish recruits as well, because playing Kim was popular in the Hebrew boy scouts.

The problem with creating Kims, as Ben-Nahum observed, is that Kim is a myth. He's no more real than Mowgli, the other famous boy from Kipling. You can't really be raised by wolves, and you can't really become someone else. An identity is made up of thousands of tiny hints, and an outsider isn't going to get them all right. A Croat might pretend to be a Russian in Venezuela but wouldn't get away with it in Russia. It would be hard even in your own country: an urban American from Chicago, for example, sent to rural Kentucky to pass as a local would probably find that despite sharing a language and a nationality he wouldn't fool people for long. When Leigh Fermor and Hammond of the Special Operations Executive were dropped among Greek partisans to organize the resistance, they wore sheepskin coats and mustaches and sang Greek songs. But they knew that while a German soldier at a checkpoint might fall for the act, a real Greek never would.

But here in Palestine was a unique circumstance—a reservoir of people who could pass perfectly for dozens of nationalities from Bukhara to Buenos Aires. In the case of the Jews, Ben-Nahum writes, "ethnic impersonation isn't a military doctrine used by sophisticated generals intent on victory, but the survival method of a persecuted wanderer who concealed his origins to save his life."

If you wanted to impersonate Germans to fight the Germans, the Jews had people who could actually do it. During the panic of 1941, in a forest outside Kibbutz Mishmar Ha'emek, the Special Operations Executive and the Palmach trained a group of fighters meant to disrupt a Nazi occupation of Palestine. One of the men remembered it like this: "In the evenings we sat around the camp-fire and sang German songs. Our camp was truly a German military camp. We lived in a cave that we decorated with German symbols and flags. When we had parties, we put on German plays." If you approached the cave, you'd be halted by soldiers in Nazi uniform. All the soldiers were German Jews. This was the "German Section."

Double identity has always been part of life for Jews, members of a minority often outwardly indistinguishable from the majority. You wonder how much to show or hide at different times, how the sides of you fit, and whether it's possible to abandon one side altogether. Some of the oldest stories told by Jews about themselves feature characters who use their double nature at crucial moments to aid their people among the greater nations that threaten it. One story has a girl with the Hebrew name Hadassah, who lives in Persia and also has a Persian name, Esther, and who wins a beauty contest and becomes queen in time to avert a genocide plotted by the royal vizier. She has been put in place, we are to understand, by a kind of divine operational plan beyond her perception. In the book of Exodus we meet Moses, a son of Hebrew slaves who is raised as an Egyptian prince and who can thus maneuver in the palace at the crucial moment of the Exodus. There's the boy Joseph, who rises in Pharaoh's court as an official named Zofnat-Paaneah, and who becomes so like an Egyptian that when his own brothers escape a famine in Canaan and come begging for food they don't recognize him. Joseph toys with them, accusing them of deceiving him, and then, making explicit one of the implicit threads of these stories, he accuses them of being spies.

In the real world, this characteristic has fed the idea that Jews are tricking everyone with their appearance while reporting to a secret conspiracy—that is, that they're all a kind of spy. People often fear or distrust others who don't resemble them, such as people with a different skin color. But another kind of unease is stirred by someone who looks like you but isn't you. We might remember poor Alfred Dreyfus, the Jewish officer convicted wrongly of treason in France in 1894. Dreyfus believed himself to be a Frenchman, but it turned out that much of France believed that he wasn't a Frenchman at all but an alien who had somehow made himself seem French, and that this insidious threat to their identity must be eradicated. Over the centuries of Jewish life among other nations, different programs have been undertaken toward this eradication. The most effective of them was being pursued by Germany in Europe precisely as the Arab Section formed in Palestine in 1941.

The curses that always came with the Jews' multiple identities and languages led the Zionist movement to try to replace it all with one language, Hebrew, and one identity, which would come to be called Israeli. The idea was to normalize this strange people. But for spies their abnormality was a gift.

Facing the German advance in 1941, the British special operations officers needed agents who could operate in Syria and Lebanon, which were ruled by the collaborationist government of Vichy France and expected to soon fall behind German lines. With the Arab world firmly in the German camp, recruiting locals was hard. But here too the Jewish "Friends" turned out to have something to offer. These were people on the fringes of Jewish society in Palestine, people to whom few paid much attention at the time, because they didn't seem like Jews at all. They seemed like Arabs.

The unit's first incarnation, the Syrian Section, operated for a time under British tutelage. The early training, to judge from a few surviving photographs in the Palmach archive, was in the spirit of Lawrence of Arabia:

A handful of agents were dispatched in less fanciful costumes into Syria and Lebanon and spent time there undercover. But when the threat of invasion passed after the Nazi reversal at El-Alamein in 1942, the operation was rendered irrelevant. By 1943 the Allies had gained the upper hand in the war, the panic in Palestine subsided, and the British and Jews remembered why they'd been at odds before. The Syrian Section was dismantled.

But the commanders of the Palmach, now operating illegally outside British control, were wise enough to know the value of the Ones Who Become Like Arabs. They understood that the unit had to be preserved. They housed its members, perhaps twenty of them at most, in an obscure ruin in a corner of the Carmel range. Sam'an, who'd been recruited by the British but was now working as an Arabic teacher, was called back by the Palmach to take over as chief instructor. He got rid of the men whose Arab identities were inadequate, of whom there seem to have been many, and replaced them with new agents like Isaac and Gamliel, forming the Section as it existed at the beginning of the Independence War and at the beginning of our story.

That was how the Ones Who Become Like Arabs ended up using their complicated Jewish selves as a weapon to create a place where their selves could be less complicated—a country whose children wouldn't be like Poles, or Russians, or Arabs, or like anyone but themselves. And that was how two young strangers appeared on a deserted street near the docks in Arab Haifa at the beginning of May 1948, just after the fall of the city and the flight of most of its Arab inhabitants, and just before the invasion of five Arab armies presented the Jews with a threat even more dire than the one they'd faced so far.

11: Exceptional Opportunities

The newly declassified files at Israel's military archive contain a memo circulated in the Jewish command in early May:

Subject: "The Dawn"
I didn't have time to speak with you about this.
We must not miss the exceptional opportunities to insert men
from The Dawn into the flow of refugees, aiming them toward
enemy forces and particularly toward neighboring countries.
The council demands a small budget for this, and also
instruction regarding the destination, the goal, and so forth.
We must act without delay. . . .
Hillel. *

It hadn't been two weeks since the battle in Haifa, and the Arab sector was already a "carcass city," in the words of one visitor. The streets were nearly empty except for stray cats.

A small group of women, children, and old people were sitting with packs on one of the streets near the harbor, waiting for a bus to take them through the battle lines to the Lebanon border and

---

* Hillel was the code name of Yisrael Galili, a member of the Zionist leadership with responsibility for defense.

then to Beirut. The bus was parked nearby, but the driver had gone off somewhere until more passengers showed up, or until these ones agreed to pay more—this kind of risky trip wasn't cheap. The two strangers appeared from somewhere and sat down. They were both in their early twenties, and they both had mustaches. The one with round glasses said he'd seen action in the war against the Jews and was now going to join the armies massing for the invasion. That was Abdul Karim, or Isaac.

The second man was the port worker with the bullet hole in his cap, the one who'd seen the *Exodus* arrive, who'd been detained by troops who put him in a truck, and who went by the name Ibrahim. He'd chosen that name himself. The one his parents gave him upon his birth in Yemen was Havakuk. That name belonged to the Hebrew Bible's most obscure prophet, author of these lines:

> I will stand on my watch,
> Take up my station at the post,
> And wait to see what He will say to me,
> What He will reply to my complaint.

> The Lord answered me and said:
> Write the prophecy down,
> Inscribe it clearly on tablets,
> So that it can be read easily.
> For there is yet a prophecy for a set term,
> A truthful witness for a time that will come.

The prophet's namesake in the Arab Section was a truthful witness, a watcher of exceptional sensitivity. After nearly having his cover blown by a soldier who recognized him, Havakuk had managed to make his way back to the Section and leave a report describing how he'd just experienced the Jewish conquest of Haifa from the Arab side. The report's vivid content and its tone, at once dispassionate and empathetic, make it one of the most striking documents from the 1948 war.

Havakuk/Ibrahim had spent months planted in Haifa in two long stints. The loneliness and the strain of constant lying almost broke him more than once. The worst moments were Friday nights, the eve of the Sabbath, when he was alone at the flophouse: "A terrible mood would attack me," he recorded, "as I thought about my friends sitting at their tables, their faces joyful, singing and carousing." Sometimes he sneaked off to find a radio and listen to *As You Request*, a Hebrew music program. Once he even left the Arab sector and went up the slopes of Mount Carmel to a Jewish neighborhood to see a friend from his real life, sitting with him in a café and speaking Hebrew. This was a grave breach of the rules, even if the rules weren't clear in those days, and when the commanders found out he was reprimanded and didn't try that again.

Though the Section's men usually went in and out of Arab areas on quick missions disguised as itinerant workers, barbers, or peddlers, the plan was to have them develop deeper cover and establish themselves inside Arab society. This would allow them to get better information and save them the perilous crossings back and forth. The guinea pig was the volatile Yakuba, who was planted at the Haifa port for a time as a laborer from the Syrian region of Houran, killing lice with the other workers, suffering the abuse of the Palestinian Arab foreman, pilfering almonds and dates from sacks he loaded, and sleeping on the rancid floor of fish stores shuttered for the night. After a few weeks, the agent's sanity began to slip. "There were days," Yakuba remembered, "when I thought,

Maybe the whole story about the Palmach, and my childhood in Jerusalem, maybe it's all a dream. Maybe I'm really a Hourani." He broke after three months and had to beg to come home. One thing that made Yakuba angry was the commanders' idea that Arab cover meant poverty and dirt, "eating straw and shit and working like a dog," as he put it. He thought this was a caricature.

Another agent planted at the Dead Sea chemical works couldn't last and had to be pulled out right away. But Havakuk persisted in Haifa until the city fell, then came back out and reported. Now, accompanied by Isaac, he was headed even deeper into enemy territory.

Both of the spies looked haggard. They'd just been released from an improvised jail in a cave outside Haifa where the Hagana was keeping Arab suspects, and where the two of them were held to improve their cover. Only the officer in charge knew who they were, not the guards. When they were led in, blindfolded, a guard kicked Isaac in the back so hard that he fell and had to force himself not to yell. He swore that if it happened again he'd turn around and shout *yob tvoyu mat*, the worst Russian curse he'd learned from the Ashkenazim on the kibbutz, something he thought would make an impression on the guard. He didn't care that it would blow his cover. But the guard turned around and left him there.

The two prisoners spent a few days crowded into the cave with thirty other men, using a single bucket for a toilet, sleeping back-to-back in case other prisoners jumped them in the dark. They endured real interrogations conducted by two Arabic-speaking Jews. After Isaac gave his cover story, the man asking the questions turned to his partner, switched to Hebrew, and said: This bastard is a liar. Which was true, and suggests that the Jews may have been better interrogators than spies.

In the end the two of them were blindfolded again and taken to a waiting car, sliding into the backseat as the Arab prisoners Ibrahim and Abdul Karim and stepping out after a short drive as Havakuk and Isaac of the Arab Section. They found themselves at Teltsch House, which used to run notices advertising itself as Haifa's "most beautiful and well-appointed hotel," located in a pine forest on the western slope of Mount Carmel just a six-minute drive from the beach, but which was now an austere military headquarters running the battles in and around Haifa. One of the Section commanders was waiting for them.

There was no farewell party and no briefing. Thousands were dead across the country, thousands more would die, the Jews were bracing for the invasion of the Arab states, and everyone was preoccupied. Their destination was Beirut, but they'd have to figure out how to get there. They had no radio and no other way to communicate. The Section would find them somehow, if the Jews held out. The officer gave them some money and handed Isaac a small pistol. Good luck, the officer said, and that was it. The two spies grasped *the idea*, as the old Palmach parable went, setting off on foot down the steep streets toward the Arab sector at the bottom of the hill, assuming their Arab identities as they walked. It would be a very long time before they'd revert to themselves.

They reached the streets near the docks and found the group of refugees waiting to leave. When the nearby bus showed no sign of movement, Isaac went to look for the driver and found him having a leisurely drink with a few other men nearby.

Why are these people sitting on the sidewalk and not being allowed on the bus? Isaac asked, gesturing toward the refugees. No good answer was forthcoming. Isaac took the driver's hand and placed it on the breast of his jacket so the man could feel the hard L of the pistol through the fabric.

I'm from the jihad in Jaffa, said Isaac / Abdul Karim. Do me a favor.

Soon they were all rolling past empty shops and homes, out of the desolate city and into the Galilee countryside. Before long they reached a checkpoint manned by soldiers from a force of foreign volunteers called the Arab Liberation Army, which had already moved into Palestine without waiting for the British departure. This army was commanded by Fawzi al-Qawuqji, who'd promised to wage "total war" against the Jews and to "murder, wreck, and ruin everything in our way." The Arab Liberation Army's emblem was a Star of David with a dagger through it.

The Arab soldiers flagged down the bus, and a pair of them stepped on, scanned the passengers' faces, and called aside the two young men they spotted among the passengers. Men of military age weren't supposed to be running away.

We leave our homes, our wives, and our children to help you fight the Jews, and you're leaving your own land and escaping? one of the soldiers spat at Isaac.

The spy showed his pistol. If this gun had a mouth, Isaac said, it would tell you how many Jews I've killed.

The soldier wanted to know why he was leaving.

The Jews killed my father, Isaac said, making it up as he went along, and my mother took my little brothers and sisters to her family in Aleppo. Isaac usually inserted Aleppo into his cover story, in case a listener picked up traces of his native dialect.

Because I'm the firstborn, I'm responsible for them, Isaac said. I need to make sure they're safe. But I'll be back to fight.

The soldiers waved them through, and the bus drove toward
the Lebanon border, passing through fields still green at the end
of the rainy season. Unlike the other passengers, our two weren't
fleeing to safety but traveling into greater danger. Like everyone
else, though, they didn't know where they'd end up, or if they'd
ever be back.

12: The Fall of Israel

When the bus crossed northward out of Palestine and into Lebanon, the spies were greeted by the alarming sight of huge military convoys driving in the opposite direction, moving into position for the Arab offensive. There were troop trucks, artillery pieces, and armored vehicles. The only soldiers they'd ever seen with arms like that were the British. The heaviest weapon they'd ever fired themselves was a rifle. The Palmach, the best force the Jews could field, seemed pathetic in comparison.

Perhaps Havakuk thought about Mira, the fighter he was leaving behind. She'd spent the past few months as an armed convoy escort up to Jerusalem, riding atop vegetable crates with her Sten, passing the burnt-out cars of previous convoys ambushed on the road. It was a dangerous job, and as if that weren't bad enough, the kibbutz where she lived in Galilee, the one where the two of them had met at a campfire, was now threatened by the Arab Liberation Army. When the invasion order came these new armies would be moving in her direction.

I met Mira when she was eighty-five, a slight and formidable woman with a hoarse voice. She lived on the same kibbutz, Alonim. I asked her whether she'd lost faith at that moment in May 1948. She said no. She was seventeen, and she knew the Palmach couldn't lose. "You couldn't do anything but believe in these people who were giving everything they had," she said. "They were together—all for one and one for all. They went together and came back together." On the Palestine-Lebanon frontier, looking at the Arab staging areas out the bus window, her boyfriend was less certain. The fighters didn't always come back together, or at all. Mira knew that, because she had a brother named Ben-Zion, a Palmach machine gunner, who died in those same weeks in the battle at Nebi Samwil. And the war wasn't done with her yet.

The bus continued up the coast into Lebanon, leaving the border behind, passing the cities of Tyre and Sidon before reaching the "impossible city," as the British writer Jan Morris called it in those years:

It is impossible in the enchantment of its setting, where the Lebanese mountains meet the Mediterranean. It is impossible in its headiness of character, its irresponsible gaiety, its humid prevarications. It is impossible economically, incorrigibly prospering under a system condemned by many serious theorists as utterly unworkable. Just as the bumble bee is aerodynamically incapable of flying, so Beirut, by all the rules and precedents, has no right to exist.

Yet there it stands, with a toss of curls and a flounce of skirts, a Carmen among the cities. . . .

Here you may see the political exiles, talking dark and interminable subterfuge, or the resplendent hawk-nosed sheikhs, in all the gilded refulgence of the Arab patrimony, fingering their beads and indulging in flamboyant bickering. Here are the silken ladies of Syria, svelte and doe-eyed, and here are the waterside harlots, curled but smouldering, Semite with a touch of baroque.

Her description is so good you can't mention that incarnation of Beirut without quoting it, even if we understand that our story doesn't exist in the fanciful world of the Western correspondent, and that we won't meet a resplendent sheikh here, or anyone smouldering. Beirut was an Arab metropolis shaped by the French over years of colonial rule and still dominated by their Francophile clients, the Maronite Christians. The stern moralism of the rest of the region was harder to find in this little coastal enclave, the breezes less Arabian than Mediterranean, the atmosphere laissez-faire. It was a place set gracefully between the sea and the hills of Mount Lebanon, white-capped in the winter months, a hybrid of Thessaloníki, Damascus, and Bern.

At first the two spies were housed in a school with the other refugees, but they left quickly to avoid uncomfortable questions about their homes and relatives. They rented a room instead at a cheap hotel. The only instruction they'd been given was to take a few hours in the afternoons to walk around a downtown plaza called the Place des Martyrs and to look for a familiar face—that of their intellectual comrade, Gamliel, who'd apparently been given the same instruction before dropping out of contact earlier in the year.

When they ventured out of the hotel and into the metropolis, sticking close together, they found Beirut's streets awash in people who seemed disoriented, torn from somewhere else, like them. They made their way to the Place des Martyrs and found a chaotic rectangle full of cars and horse-drawn carts weaving around people coming from work or from the crowded old markets hidden behind the square, bits of the Middle East that had somehow survived the modern redesign of the city by French architects. There were citizens hurrying to appointments in the government offices at the Petit Serail on the north side of the rectangle, and the usual urban assortment of beggars and touts. Preserved in the intelligence files at Israel's military archives is a 1942 French map titled "Beyrouth Ville," which seems to have been used by the agents or by headquarters. This detail shows the Place des Martyrs and its environs:

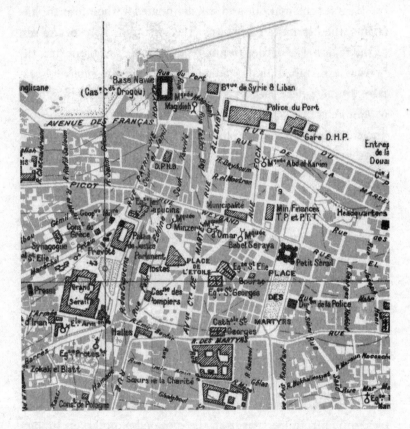

If you stayed in the Place after the workday ended, you'd see the mood shift, the offices shutting down, the cafés coming alive, the poor vanishing back to their streets on the fringes of the city, the rich and the foreigners heading for cabarets like the Black

Elephant and the Kit-Kat Club, which, according to one history of Beirut, "sought to re-create the ceremonies of the Parisian night with an admixture of oriental sensuality." This was when the action would begin in earnest on a street that one entered from the eastern side of the rectangle, named for the great Arab poet el-Mutanabbi: the red-light district, home to famous establishments like the one run by the Greek madam Marika Spiridon, whose salon regularly hosted the city's politicians and notables. The brothels operated legally and were subject to weekly health inspections by the vice squad.

Amid the crowds at the Place des Martyrs there was no sign of the familiar face they sought. They had no way to reach Gamliel or anyone else. And the influx of strangers had brought Beirut a spy fever so acute that Isaac remembers the Arabic word for "spies" being a kind of constant whisper in the air—*jawasis, jawasis.* There was a report that a certain old beggar had been revealed as a Jewish spy, and rumors that you could tell a spy by a mark on his back or inside his mouth, like a Star of David on a wisdom tooth. Such people, it was said, had been uncovered in Syria. Any stranger was suspect, and there were many strangers about.

When the Beirut police began coming around to check hotels for spies, Isaac and Havakuk decided they'd be safer renting beds in someone's home. At a storefront real estate agency, they asked for a furnished room with a family, and the clerk inquired first about their religion. He did this carefully, in the Lebanese fashion, a recognition of the explosive nature of matters like faith and ethnicity, forces that would indeed tear Lebanon apart later on. *Al-hamdulillah muslimin,* Isaac replied: Thank God, we're Muslims.

The clerk reminded them that few Muslim families would take in male boarders. It would be immodest in a house with women. But Christians would do it, the man said, and they ended up spending a few days with a Christian woman who asked too many questions. When they moved yet again, it was to a room that opened onto a courtyard with a communal toilet, the kind of poor place where Isaac grew up in Aleppo. That arrangement ended when a woman who went into the toilet after Isaac one day made a suspicious discovery: This working-class Palestinian Muslim, Abdul Karim, used toilet paper, a habit that was Western and middle class. The locals used water, as Isaac had before reaching the Land of Israel and picking up new ways.

The busybody went to Havakuk/Ibrahim, who must not have exhibited the same suspicious behavior, and asked, Who's your friend?

Why? asked Havakuk.

Something's strange about him, the woman said, mentioning the toilet paper. She thought he might be a Jewish spy.

Havakuk reassured her that he'd known Abdul Karim for years, and that his friend suffered from a medical problem that required the use of toilet paper on doctor's orders. The woman relented, but they were scared enough to move again.

Isaac had a few close calls before, but there was one in particular that haunted him then, and still does, if it's possible to judge from the care he took to tell this story. He recounted it in detail at our usual place in his kitchen, speaking with understated drama in his ninety-year-old voice. In subsequent meetings he asked me several times whether he'd already told me this story, and gave me a written version of it that he'd had his daughter type up some years before.

This incident happened before the Independence War, at a Bedouin encampment off a remote road running across the highlands west of the Sea of Galilee. He arrived on an afternoon bus and walked to the camp with an Arabic newspaper in his hand and a story about looking for livestock for his father's meat business in Jaffa. After greeting him with the requisite hospitality and serving coffee in the main tent, and after some talk about cattle, the illiterate clansmen asked him to read them an article from his newspaper, which he did. It was an article about the advancement of the Arab woman, who was now (so the article explained) making great strides in politics and education. In his opinion, the bespectacled visitor told them, warming to the role, if we have this kind of Arab woman, our nation has a future.

His hosts seemed pleased to have an educated guest. They served him meat of poor quality, hard and white, which they dipped in water to soften before eating. But this didn't throw Isaac, who'd had similar fare before. He'd just spent a few days in a nearby cattle market picking up the jargon, the right questions to ask about cows and goats: Does she still calve? Does she have milk? How are her teeth?

After dinner a new man ducked into the tent. He had a long white beard, and everyone deferred to him. This was the clan's sheikh. He saw through Isaac right away.

Where are you from? the sheikh asked. Jaffa? Where's your father's shop?

Opposite the mosque, said Isaac / Abdul Karim. He mentioned the names of two other shops he knew in Jaffa, and said his father's shop was between them. What could a rural Bedouin know about the big city?

The sheikh paused. I know that part of Jaffa like the palm of my hand, he said. There's no store like the one you're describing.

It had grown dark outside. The clansmen gathered around the two of them, their interest in Isaac now assuming a different cast. Blending in with an Arab crowd in a city was one thing. This was another. For a few moments, Isaac went quiet as a corpse.

Look, he said, struggling to remain calm. If I say now that the store does exist, it will be interpreted as my saying that the old man, who's the age of my own grandfather, is a liar. So it would be better for me to be the liar and for him to be right.

It was a good answer, but the old man spoke again.

Son, he said, you're here under our protection. If you're running away from the police, from jail, from your family, from some problem, you'll be safe here. If you want us to smuggle you to Syria, Lebanon, Jordan, just say so—we have horses. Two of our men will escort you wherever you want to go. Only, in God's name, don't tell us this story about the cattle.

The man knew Isaac was lying. Isaac knew he knew. But if he changed his story he'd be lost. After a while, some of the men took him to another tent on the outskirts of the camp and left him there. He saw lights twinkling on nearby hills—Jewish villages. He could make a run for it. But he was afraid that the Bedouin had put him in that tent on purpose to see if he'd run, and that they'd jump him as soon as he moved. He pretended to sleep and just lay there wondering what would happen. A few hours later someone shook him and demanded his identity card. Isaac handed over the slip of paper identifying him as Abdul Karim Muhammad Sidki.

In the morning a few clansmen came and handed back the card. He was free to go. As for livestock—they had nothing to sell. Maybe they believed him after all. Or maybe, as seems more likely, they just didn't want to take him captive or kill him, which would have brought the tribe more trouble than Isaac was worth. Instead they released him to grasp the stakes of the game he'd joined and the fact that he wasn't good enough.

WITHIN TWO WEEKS of the spies' arrival in Beirut, on May 14, Britain's last High Commissioner for Palestine arrived at the Haifa port, boarded HMS *Euryalus*, and sailed away for good. The Union Jack came down, three decades of British Mandate rule ended, the Arab invasion began, and the 1948 war entered its second stage. Now the Jews were fighting not just local guerrillas but armies, from every direction, their backs to the sea.

Isaac and Havakuk had no way to find out what was happening. Their only news came from triumphant Arabic headlines on Beirut newsstands:

THE ARAB LEGION CONQUERS JERUSALEM,
REACHES ITS HEART AND ERASES
THE LAST POCKETS OF JEWISH RESISTANCE

FIRST MILITARY REPORT BROADCAST IN LEBANON:
THE LEBANESE ARMY HAS ACCOMPLISHED ITS MISSIONS

There were other reports and rumors: the Arab Liberation Army was at the gates of Haifa and preparing to seize the city back from the Jews. The Egyptians were coming up from the desert and preparing their final assault on Tel Aviv. Readers of *Beirut al-Masaa* were treated to a political caricature: a long-nosed, bearded Jewish serpent at the gate to the Al-Aqsa Mosque in Jerusalem, its head chopped off by an Arab ax.

On the day of the British departure the Jewish state was declared—that is, a proclamation was read out by David Ben-Gurion to notables crowded into a stuffy room in Tel Aviv in a ceremony lasting thirty-two minutes. The fighting outside the room was terrible, and three Jewish settlements had surrendered to Arab forces that morning. His declaration was an expression of hope, not a statement of fact. The Zionist leadership had taken a vote and decided to call their state Israel. This meant that Isaac and Havakuk had just become "Israeli." They'd also just become the first Israeli spies. But they had no idea that any of it had happened. They didn't know they had a state.

The feeling of being stranded in this way was once described by Xan Fielding, a writer who spent the Second World War with the Special Operations Executive and found himself cut off in occupied Crete: "To be out of wireless communication, as I had been for the last fortnight and more, always produced a certain sense of panic and loss, as though God had ceased to exist," he wrote. "For the invisible and distant Headquarters which were responsible for my fate had assumed in my eyes a quasi-divine power." And Fielding wasn't worried that his homeland had been overrun, as the Arab Section men were—that headquarters wasn't just out of contact but no longer existed at all. Their sense of losing God was of a different order.

In the Arabic papers the two spies saw things get worse. The armies of Iraq, Egypt, Transjordan, and Syria pushed deep into the former territory of the British Mandate, along with the Arab Liberation Army. Egyptian planes bombed Tel Aviv. The pioneers at the border kibbutzim Sha'ar Hagolan and Masada abandoned their homes and watched Syrian soldiers burn them.

ARAB ARTILLERY FOLLOWS THE EVACUATION OF
JEWISH NEIGHBORHOODS IN JERUSALEM AND
THE PURSUIT OF ESCAPEES, FOLLOWING THE
ARAB REFUSAL OF A JEWISH OFFER OF SURRENDER

THE LAST OBSTACLE BETWEEN THE JORDANIAN AND
EGYPTIAN ARMIES IS REMOVED AS THE RAMAT RACHEL
SETTLEMENT FALLS TO THE ARABS

Maybe the state would never be born. Maybe it was already dead. Maybe the teacher Sam'an was gone, and the whole Arab Section. Maybe the "Land of Israel" of the Zionist imagination was a fleeting dream, and the two of them, Isaac and Havakuk, would be left behind in the Arab world. They'd be just two more refugees.

"We looked at each other, Havakuk and I, with great worry: What's going to happen?" Isaac remembered. "What will be our fate if the Arabs really do capture Haifa, Tel Aviv, and Jerusalem? Should we stay in Beirut? On the one hand, we're not doing anything here; on the other, if we return, is there anything to return to?" He remembered the Arab invasion convoys they'd seen moving south. He thought what he read in the newspapers was probably true. Havakuk joked that he wasn't concerned, because he had a contingency plan for a Jewish defeat: "We can always go back to Palestine as Arabs," he said.

13: The Three Moons Kiosk

Finally, on one of their afternoon visits to the Place des Martyrs, they found Gamliel. The most thoughtful of our four spies had been living his lonely life as the shopkeeper Yussef el-Hamed for months without contact. We can imagine that the meeting was emotional, but none of them make much of it in their recollections. With the coming together of these three young men amid an oblivious crowd in Beirut in the early summer of 1948, the Jewish state's first foreign intelligence operation began to take shape.

There was no real hierarchy in the cell, in keeping with the anarchic culture of the Palmach. But because Gamliel had been in Beirut the longest, he took charge. They still had no orders or any idea what to do, so they went out in the evenings to eat hummus and beans, cheap dishes in workers' diners. They didn't have much money and weren't sure when more would come. The basic rules of compartmentalization meant having nothing to do with each other, but no one really knew the rules, and the three of them clung to each other anyway.

Before long, another familiar face appeared at the Place des Martyrs, an agent named Shaul/Tawfiq, who'd blended in with refugees escaping Haifa by boat. A fifth agent then reached Beirut after crossing the border overland—this was Shimon, who would soon move to Damascus to open the Section's station there.

Shimon came with an ordinary radio in an old-fashioned wooden case. Concealed inside, at last, was their transmitter.

Havakuk had been trained as a radio operator, so he took charge of the set, concealing it in a drawer in the rooftop room he'd found with Isaac. They disguised the antenna as a clothes-line. Down in Israel, in the corner of a shed at Kibbutz Givat Hashlosha, Arab Section headquarters had set up a radio on a wooden table:

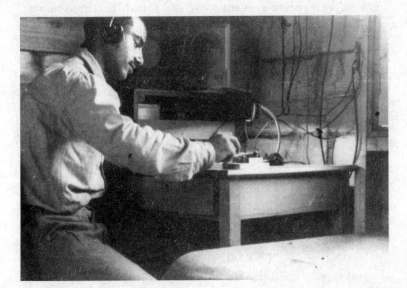

In Beirut, Havakuk sat down and began to tap. The frequency came to life.

The men in Beirut, desperate to hear the true course of the war, now heard that their new state was holding out, but with terrible losses. One of every one hundred Jews in Palestine at the beginning of the war would be dead by its end. The outcome was still uncertain. The Morse operator at headquarters sent them so many queries in the first weeks that Havakuk was tapping out answers several times a day, which increased the chances of detection. Seventeen years later, this would be the mistake that helped the Syrians catch the spy Eli Cohen in Damascus. In these early days in the summer of 1948, headquarters didn't think the Lebanese could pick up the transmissions. But they weren't sure.

The men rented rooms around town and tried to create plausible lives. Gamliel ran his sweet shop. The others bought a small kiosk by a Christian elementary school called the Three Moons. They chatted up the people they met, especially anyone connected to the army or government. Gamliel read the papers and prepared a summary, which Havakuk encoded, sending a daily message with anything worthwhile—descriptions of parliamentary debates, bellicose statements by Arab leaders, signs of rising or flagging enthusiasm for the war:

> During the session all roads leading to parliament were blocked and no one could get close to the building. In his speech [Prime Minister] Riad al-Solh discussed the subject of Palestine. . . . He hoped that if the Arabs unite they can take advantage of the unstable legal situation in Palestine and save it. The task of the Arabs today is to organize their steps, to unite in their words, and to save Palestine at any price.
>
> —The Dawn

From the shed that was Arab Section headquarters, the information went into the reports prepared by the intelligence office for the country's generals and politicians, who had to gauge the bewildering set of military threats they faced. Was Lebanon planning to strike across the border in support of the Arab cause, or just wait-ing for the war to blow over? Were the Syrians feeling confident or discouraged? There was no superagent, no secret document that held the key to events, no single stroke that solved everything. There was only a murky lake of shifting and contradictory facts.

The intelligence officers in Israel were preoccupied with the fate of the hundreds of thousands of Arab refugees from the war—how many there were, where they'd ended up, and whether they'd be resettled in the Arab world. Much was riding on the answer, because the new state wouldn't survive with a large and hostile population inside its borders allied with the hostile region outside its borders. The agents saw the camps on the outskirts of Beirut. They did their best to report how the Lebanese were treating the refugees (they were offering pity but little money) and what inter-national aid organizations were giving them (money and supplies, most of it not reaching the people in need).

The agents also described the mood in the enemy countries, which changed as the summer wore on and the Arab campaign began to sour. There were few victories to report. Now, Gamliel wrote in one dispatch, "the newspapers describe the Jew in the most barbaric and cruel fashion, and also as weak and cowardly." Many people, he reported, believed that Jews "were slaughtering children and abusing pregnant women and raping virgins." The word *Jew* was starting to assume demonic undertones.

Enthusiasm for the war was flagging, Gamliel reported, par-ticularly among Lebanon's Christians, many of whom hadn't felt strongly about it in the first place. Some Lebanese Christians saw a Jewish state as a potential ally against the Islamic world, and some described themselves not as Arab at all, but as descendants of the ancient Phoenicians. But even among the Christians, wrote

Gamliel, "it's impossible to find an influential group willing to express an opinion against the war and in favor of peace . . . because the people have been caught up in the anti-Jewish wave, and their hearts can't be won except with anti-Jewish proclamations."

In the same report he also noted an attempt at counter-espionage by the defense ministries in Lebanon and Syria. "They believe," he wrote, "that there is a large network of Lebanese Arab spies among influential and well-known people." Perhaps the officers at headquarters chuckled at this line.

Israel's first intelligence station in the Arab world revolved around the little kiosk by the Three Moons school. At dawn each morning one of the men raised the little window as the city woke up. The first customers, early morning workers, arrived not long afterward, and then came animated schoolchildren walking to the Three Moons, their hair still combed and their books in order. The spies sold pencils, erasers, soda, candy, and sandwiches. "The inside of the store is strategic for us," Isaac reported to headquarters, "because from the outside you can't see what's going on inside, and in the middle is a partition of cupboards behind which it is possible to organize and hide many things without being seen." The agents bought a regular transistor for the kiosk, and when business was slow they went behind the partition, fiddled with the dials, lowered the volume, and tried to pick up news broadcasts from the Voice of Israel.

Every morning one of them went to the wholesale market to buy cheese, buns, pickles, and cans of pâté. The kiosk made some money that helped keep the cell going, and also saved them money, because they could eat their stock instead of going to restaurants. Because they lacked the refugee cards given out by the United Nations, the agents couldn't get the food assistance granted to others displaced by the war. The spies were not, in other words, navigating candlesticks and crystal at dinner parties, or insinuating themselves into the corridors of power. Their position was like that of Russian agents tasked with gleaning intelligence not from Capitol Hill or Wall Street but from the sidewalk outside a public school in Queens.

In reports from the Section and other sources that summer and fall, Israel's intelligence collators learned that Beirut was undefended against air attack; that the Syrian army had just placed an order for one thousand binoculars; that the US-flagged merchantman *Exchange* had docked at Beirut with 112 tons of explosives, shells, light ammunition, and other matériel. A few weeks later came a shipment from Italy with Beretta submachine guns and mortars of 81- and 60-millimeter caliber. Among the goods unloaded at Beirut "which could help the war effort," according to one report, were these:

- 100 tons of leather
- 10 Peugeots
- 14,822 kilograms of car parts and 8,826 kilograms of tires and inner tubes
- Pumps
- Telephone cables
- Lightbulbs
- Mercury (100 bottles)
- 23 tons of preserved meat in cans
- 9,000 tons of American flour
- 240 tons of Finnish paper

At the Rayak airfield someone reported twelve large planes with two or four engines, but these were dummies, "left outside on purpose." There were also sixteen two-engine Dakotas, which were real, but next to this point in the document someone in the intelligence office penciled a question mark. It was so hard to say what was real.

The files contain a package that Gamliel somehow smuggled to Israel, with a map of Beirut and a list of potential targets. At coordinates 1326021835, for example, were the Shell petroleum stores, and at 1298821835 were "large customs warehouses full of supplies." He also listed a streetcar garage, the Officers' Club, a radio tower, the home of the prime minister, the Presidential Palace, the Defense Ministry, and the UNESCO building. At 1319021714, he noted, was "an iron bridge that could easily be destroyed with a cone bomb."

As the spies settled into their false lives and as their information accrued in the Israeli files, headquarters became more worried about the level of their tradecraft. The men in Beirut had never been professionally trained, or prepared for the complexity and danger of a mission like this. Neither had the people at headquarters. They were frequently careless. The records make clear that the agents not only knew each other and knew the real name and alias of each member of the cell but also spent a lot of time together, which would make it much easier to catch them all. The rich photo archives of the Palmach show that they'd bought a camera and frequently used it to photograph not just subjects of intelligence interest but also themselves.

Messages in the log show the teacher Sam'an and others trying to instill caution and discipline. This was hard to do over the radio, especially with men who were products of the insouciant chaos of the Palmach, but the commanders tried. The radio transmissions usually began and ended with the same words, for example, and someone finally realized this was foolish—repetitive phrases were gifts to code breakers, the kind of thing that helped the British teams at Bletchley Park crack the Nazis' Enigma encryption a few years before. So this had to change:

> Because of the possibility that the enemy can listen in on our broadcasts and crack our code, from tomorrow there is a new instruction: We will no longer say "Gamliel from The Dawn" and "The Dawn to Gamliel," or the ending that is always used, "Be strong." The telegram should begin without the addressee, and the ending should change each time.

A few days later this came in from headquarters:

> The enemy has a listening station that they're using against us, and we could be exposed.

It occurred to someone that the electricity used by the radio might draw the attention of the meter reader from the electric company. Headquarters recommended that Havakuk buy an appliance, perhaps a kettle, to serve as a plausible explanation for the electricity bill if the apartment was searched.

But the most effective warning came one evening a few of them went to a cinema to relax. Before the feature came a newsreel about the war in Palestine. There was footage of the Egyptian expeditionary force, and then of an Egyptian police station at Gaza. In front of the building were two men, bound, their clothes in tatters, eyes down. These two, announced the newsreel narrator, were Zionist spies caught by the Egyptian army. But the agents in the theater knew that already. They'd frozen with horror in their seats. It was Dahud and Ezra of the Arab Section:

Dahud was the married one, whose wife was now pregnant. Ezra was the one known for comic relief, and for asking the others to torture him so he'd be steeled for the real thing when it came. The two men flickered on the screen for just a few moments, but it was enough. Ezra's grin was gone, and he had blue marks under his eyes. The pair had cover as Arab villagers fleeing the Jews, but it didn't get them far. An Egyptian communiqué said they were caught near an army camp with a jar containing typhus and dysentery bacteria, and the Arab press was calling them the "well poisoners." The Egyptians tortured them, extracted written confessions, and shot them. Of the dozen or so Arab Section agents active at the beginning of the Independence War, five were now dead.

14: Casino Méditerranée

One of our four spies was still missing in the early fall of 1948—the volatile Yakuba. He was still in Israel. He'd been held back to learn to use new explosives, some recently arrived in shipments from Czechoslovakia and others developed by Israeli scientists, like cone-shaped bombs that could blow through doors and walls.

Yakuba was just twenty-four, but he'd been in the Section for six years, longer than any of the others. Explosives, and mayhem more generally, were considered his department. He'd carried out the garage bombing with Isaac, as you'll remember, and a string of actions with the Palmach before that. During an operation that came to be known as the Night of the Bridges, when the fighters blew up transport links across Palestine to paralyze the British, he'd fought a man hand to hand on a bridge over the Jordan and drove a knife into his opponent's throat. He was also one of three fighters responsible for the Palmach's best-known vigilante operation in the early years: they went into the Arab town of Beisan in disguise, seized a man suspected of raping several Jewish women in the Jordan Valley, drugged him, and castrated him. This was around 1943. The rapes stopped, and the operation was celebrated for a time around Palmach campfires, though it isn't mentioned now. People know how it sounds. Yakuba didn't celebrate violence.

Sometimes, as in the incident with the rapist, it made him sick. But he understood it was his job.

One day that fall he was finally summoned to a military head-quarters in Tel Aviv. In the midst of the fighting, the old Hagana, the underground organization of which the Palmach was part, had morphed into the beginnings of a real army, the Israel Defense Forces. This army had an intelligence branch. The apparatus wasn't yet divided into the distinct arms that would exist later—military intelligence, Shin Bet for internal security, Mossad for activities abroad—and it was all run by an officer known as Big Isser, who was waiting for Yakuba with four large crates.*

Listen, the officer said. You're crossing to the other side. I want operations. I want missions. I want terror attacks. I want to pin them down and paralyze them, keep them busy, drive them crazy.

Absolutely, the young agent said.

I trust you, said Big Isser, and then, with irony that may or may not have been intentional, he said, Go in peace.

In the crates were explosives, pistols, and a radio intended for the second station planned for Damascus. There was a new Czech Parabellum for Yakuba and £10,000 for the Beirut cell, more money than the kid from the Jerusalem slum had ever seen.

The borders between Palestine and the neighboring Arab states were now sealed, so the agent and his cargo were to be delivered in a nighttime sortie by the Israeli navy. The navy, like the state itself, was just a few months old and more aspiration than reality—a few modest vessels, some found leaking at anchor in the Haifa port when the British left, all of them with previous lives. The navy

---

* Isser Be'eri, known as Big Isser to differentiate him from another Isser in the intelligence service, Isser Harel, known as Little Isser.

ship *Eilat*, for example, had once been the American icebreaker *Northland*, the *Hatikva* a cutter of the US Coast Guard, and the *Hagana* a Canadian corvette.

At the Haifa docks the spy boarded a small cutter formerly belonging to the British, now named *Palmach*. Inside he saw his crates already loaded on a dinghy that would be launched when they arrived at the drop-off point. After dark they sailed out to sea, and Yakuba was on the move again into the unknown. It was like his great adventure as a child, the time he took a friend and walked from Jerusalem through the Judaean desert all the way to the Dead Sea—a famous incident in his neighborhood a decade before, when he was still living at home by the vegetable market with his twelve siblings and Persian parents among Jews from Urfa and Kurdistan. He'd never seen the Dead Sea and had no map, just a vague idea of the direction, and it was miles and miles through the wilderness, and they could have died of thirst or heatstroke, but they made it. They actually swam in the strange salty basin amid the barren hills, the lowest point on the earth's surface, two boys without their parents. Then they caught a ride home with one of the trucks from the phosphate plant near Sodom, and when they got back no one believed they'd done it. They were convinced only when Yakuba took off his undershirt and it was so salty it stood up by itself. It was a real exploit, worth the punishment.

Yakuba was punished often, and sometimes when things got too bad at home he'd run off to Sheikh Badr, the Arab village on the other side of the Valley of the Cross, where he had some friends, and he'd sleep there until things calmed down. Between the Muslim kids from Sheikh Badr and the Jewish kids from the neighborhood, all of whom spoke Arabic, he picked up the language, and after he joined the Palmach someone noticed this, and also, perhaps, his affinity for action and theater. They steered him into the Arab Section. It's possible to sense Yakuba's natural abilities in a photograph of him from the early days as a Palestinian Arab militiaman:

Once the vessel crossed into hostile Lebanese waters on the night in question, it was a short distance to a point off the coast at Ouzai. The navy had arranged everything with Isaac, who was supposed to be there with one or two of the others, signaling with a flashlight. They would all bury the crates in the sand, then make a quick escape into the city. But when the sailors peered at the coast from their position offshore, they saw no figures and no flashes. The men on shore had mixed up one of the details, either the time or the location. It wasn't as if they'd ever done something like this before. The ship waited for an hour, bobbing in the waves, and when the sailors still saw nothing the order came to return to Haifa.

Yakuba wouldn't hear of it. There was no way he was going home, he said. He didn't care if anyone was waiting on the beach, or if anyone came with him—he'd go alone.

After an argument with headquarters over the ship's radio, he had his way. The dinghy was lowered with two sailors, one machine gunner, and Yakuba with his crates. They rowed ashore. When the hull scraped the sand, Yakuba jumped out as if he knew what he was doing. Walking a few paces in the dark to find a feature that would help him locate the cache afterward, he encountered the corner of a fenced-in plot that may have been an orchard. That would do. He and the two sailors started digging while the machine gunner stood guard. The crash of the surf was enough to drown out the noise of the shovels, or so they hoped, but the sailors were afraid—they were Ashkenazim and the agent felt bad for them, because if something went wrong he might blend in with the locals but they'd have no chance. They were so nervous that before they'd even finished burying the last of the four crates, Yakuba told them to go. They jumped into the dinghy and rowed back out to the ship, leaving him alone in Lebanon.

He was in the fourth hole, scooping sand from the bottom to make it deeper, when a light blinked on near the fence he'd seen—not an electric light but the softer yellow of a kerosene lantern held aloft by a human shape in a nightgown. About thirty yards separated the spy from the man with the light. Now Yakuba noticed that there was a house in the orchard, that the spot wasn't as deserted as he'd thought. The man must have heard them digging. Yakuba crouched inside the hole, drew his pistol, and froze. The man waited at his fence, peering out at the beach. After a while he went back inside, having concluded that he was mistaken or that dark figures digging on the beach at night might best be left alone.

The agent stood up, shoved the last crate into its hole, covered it with a few inches of sand, and started walking inland. He'd been given a backup rendezvous point in case something went wrong, the Casino Méditerranée in Beirut proper. But he had to make it by 2:00 a.m., when the casino closed, and it was nearly two already.

He reached the coastal highway that ran near the beach and started walking along the asphalt. There was some traffic despite the hour, and every time a car passed he jumped into the ditch on the roadside and crouched with his pistol drawn. He'd just come from the war in Palestine and didn't yet grasp that here in Lebanon things were peaceful, that the thing to do wasn't to draw a gun but to play it cool. After a while it was clear that he wasn't anywhere near the city center and wasn't going to make it if he walked. Yakuba wasn't easily thrown, as he'd demonstrated at the Abu Sham garage. He stood up straight at the side of the road, and when a cab approached he flagged it down. Now he was the refugee Jamil Muhammad Rushdi of Haifa, Palestine.

To the Casino Méditerranée as fast as possible, he told the driver. There was a woman waiting for him at the casino, he added, indulging his flair for embellishment, and using a word that suggested this woman might be less than entirely respectable. He said she'd leave at two if he wasn't there on time. The taxi driver tore north along the beach, rounding the point at Ras Beirut and pulling up at the casino with a few minutes to spare.

Yakuba didn't want to go through the main entrance, because he was afraid that if anyone searched him they'd find the pistol and the £10,000 in his pockets. So he went around the side and crawled through a hedge, finding himself near an outdoor dance floor. A short distance away he saw someone standing by the exit, waiting to settle his bill on his way out. It was Gamliel, and behind him was Shimon, the agent who'd brought the radio. They'd given up on Yakuba and were about to leave.

Yakuba sneaked up behind them and slapped their backs with a hearty Arabic *sabah el-kheir*—Good morning! They jumped, some relieved hugging followed, and then some careful and confused conversation. That was how the final agent reached Beirut.

Yakuba, in keeping with his character, seems to have wasted no time. Within a few weeks he'd found an apartment near the Saint-Michel beach, bought an Oldsmobile, and arranged to have it certified as a taxi. Before long he was ferrying passengers back and forth on the north-south line from Beirut to Tripoli. The job made them a bit of money, and provided both a chance to chat up passengers and good cover for driving around the country:

The other men also used the Oldsmobile, as we see in pictures like this one of Isaac in the driver's seat, having finally figured out how to shift gears, with Havakuk beside him:

After a few months on the Tripoli route, Yakuba began working on the east-west line from Beirut to Damascus, which provided more passengers as well as access to the Syrian capital, but also meant risking the checkpoint at the Lebanon-Syria border. Yakuba wasn't deterred. He found that his movement was eased by keeping a stack of dirty magazines on the passenger's seat; the soldiers leaning in through the car window invariably found them interesting and were happy to accept one as a gift. Thus did the refugee Jamil become one more enterprising young man around Beirut, his speech glib and friendly, his origins elusive.

There was a second arrival in Beirut at the same time, as it happened, also by sea, also of mysterious character, complex history, and uncertain motivations—a yacht with a spectral captain. And it was in these same weeks in the fall of 1948 that the Israelis decided to attempt their first act of complex sabotage beyond the border.

15: Hitler's Yacht

In the black days early in the Second World War eight years before, with Nazi forces poised to invade Britain, the Kriegsmarine prepared plans for the Führer's triumphant arrival up the Thames aboard an armed yacht built for him in the Hamburg shipyards. *Aviso Grille* was 443 feet long with cannon, antiaircraft guns, and perks not common in ships of the line: "Hitler's suite was the main attraction, with an ante-room, a bedroom and a bathroom," the journalist Revel Barker wrote in a history of the ship, the floors carpeted, the chairs and sofa "upholstered in eggshell-blue." Nearby was an identical suite but in red, rumored to be used by Hitler's mistress Eva Braun. The rumor seems to have been incorrect, according to Barker, but other notable Reich personalities spent time on board, including Göring, Hess, Goebbels, and Himmler. The *Grille* had a special detail of sailors who wore white dress uniforms and had to be at least six feet tall.

Denied her moment of glory in London, the yacht resurfaced only once more as a notable player in the world war, as the vessel aboard which Grand Admiral Dönitz announced Hitler's death in 1945 and took over as leader of the doomed Nazi state. After that it was forgotten until a burst of coded radio traffic in the Middle East three years later.

The action against the "Grille" is set by the army's general staff and we can't change it. The mission will be carried out by a member of our section who has been given special training in seaborne sabotage.

We are not entrusting you with the swimming mission because the problems are many and special training is required. The swimmer is comrade Rika. Make sure to take care of him if he has to stay longer in Lebanon.

The State of Israel would go on to earn a reputation for operations of this kind, but it began here. We've already briefly met the saboteur "comrade Rika," who left the description of what it was like to arrive at the Arab Section camp, with the gramophone and backgammon. Rika was eighteen. He'd left his home in Damascus four years earlier and followed the familiar route into the Arab Section—first a kibbutz to become like a sabra, then an encounter with the teacher Sam'an, then the tents of the Ones Who Become Like Arabs.

The message with the name of the saboteur arrived on November 17. Two days later, headquarters had a few questions. A reconnaissance plane had taken photos the previous week—an extravagance in those days, and a sign that the Israelis were using all the tools they had. The aerial photos showed the *Grille* anchored parallel to the pier in Beirut's harbor. Was that still the case? And was the light in the shore tower still on all night? Another photograph of the ship, this one taken from the ground, can be found in the Palmach archive:

The agents were to use the Oldsmobile taxi and await the saboteur at Ouzai, the same point on the coast where Yakuba had landed the previous month. They didn't need to use the explosives Yakuba brought, which the cell had reburied nearby in waterproof canisters—the saboteur would bring his own. On the day of the operation, they were to report if sea conditions allowed the mission to proceed, and then begin signaling from shore with a flashlight, switching it on for thirty seconds every fifteen minutes.

If you've read many accounts of spy exploits, and stories of Israeli operations later on, it might be possible to overlook how daunting this all was at the time. The Israelis had to communicate with a cell of agents inside enemy territory and arrange a rendezvous by sea. A saboteur had to be trained and equipped, and he had to be able to blend in with the local population if something went wrong, which is why an Arab Section man was used. The frogman needed up-to-date information on the target, hence the aerial photograph. A few months earlier, there had been no Israeli navy, army, or air force, and the spies hadn't even owned a radio. If later on the *Aviso Grille* attack was remembered by the Arab Section as "the jewel of our operations beyond the border," the appraisal was less about the results than about seeing whether the Jews could pull off something like this at all.

> Confirm that you understand everything. Answer all questions clearly tomorrow in our next contact. You will receive more details about the mission in the coming days.
> Be strong!

EVIDENCE OF NAZI fingerprints on the Arab side always drew special attention from the Jewish intelligence services. One file from July 1948, for example, includes a sighting of German Tiger tanks in the service of the Egyptian army in Gaza. Another file reports the arrival of twenty-five Wehrmacht officers, "experts on artillery, tanks and air warfare," and notes rumors that twenty-five hundred former German soldiers and Italian paratroopers would soon join them. Some of the reports, like the latter, were fanciful, but others were true. There really were German advisers working with Arab troops, and the best explosives expert among the Palestinian Arabs, the one responsible for the deadliest truck bombs of 1948, had been trained in Nazi Germany. The Palestinian Arab leader himself, the Mufti of Jerusalem, had been a prominent accomplice of Hitler's regime throughout the Second World War, broadcasting propaganda aimed at the Arab world and enlisting Muslim soldiers in the Nazi cause.

All of this supported the Jews' suspicion that links existed between the powerful forces arrayed against them. It is in this context that Israeli intelligence understood a letter intercepted that fall, written by a German who was now serving the Arab cause. According to this letter, there were twenty escaped German POWs in Beirut, and most of them were "working on the *Grille*, the Führer's private yacht."

From that moment the ship anchored at Beirut's harbor had Israel's full attention. The yacht, it turned out, now belonged to a Lebanese businessman who'd bought it from a British scrapyard after the German surrender. Beirut wasn't to be her final stop; the Israelis had information that the ship was bound for the service of King Farouk of Egypt, and that new armaments were being installed on board. The *Grille* wasn't much by the standards of the Second World War, but here it was dangerous. Israel's fleet being what it was—mainly wishful thinking—the Israeli navy feared the new ship could "significantly increase the forces of the Egyptian navy and pose a special danger in the naval arena of the Land of Israel." That appraisal is from the navy's official history of the 1948 war and was the official reason for what followed. But it wasn't the only reason.

Only two and a half years had passed since the Nazi surrender. The Jews were still trying to grasp the scope of what had happened in Europe, and to figure out who was alive. People in Israel gathered around the radio in those days to hear a show called the *Search Bureau for Missing Relatives*, whose announcer would read out a heartbreaking note from a mother looking for her daughter, or the name of a sibling last seen near Lodz in 1942, or a plea from a resident of some Hungarian hamlet looking for someone, anyone, from her town. For many, the war wasn't really over. No one was even sure that Hitler was dead.

The saboteur Rika described the discovery of Hitler's yacht in Beirut like this: "It was as if the tormentor, in his grave, hadn't come to terms with the existence of the State of Israel, and sent his personal warship against it." Gamliel pictured the ship aflame, sinking slowly into the depths. The idea, he wrote, "had the sweet taste of revenge."

Gamliel from The Dawn:
Due to moon and sea conditions it is possible that the mission will be delayed from Thursday to Sunday the twenty-eighth (28) of November. We will give you a final answer tomorrow.
Here are further instructions.
The flashlight signal should begin at 21:15 and end at 23:15.
After the man lands on the beach, the ship will sail back out to sea. It will return to the same spot two hours later. . . .
If the man isn't back on board by 04:30, the ship will return to Israel. The man will stay in Beirut until we can arrange his return.
Prepare him a set of clothes Havakuk's size, a long winter coat, a wallet and Lebanese currency, a bottle of rum, and light food.

When Isaac went to look around the harbor, it was clear something was happening on board the *Grille*: parts of the deck were covered in tarp, and strangers were kept away. There was a man near the port who rented out a *hasakeh*, a long surfboard that you paddled standing up with a double-bladed oar, and Isaac and Havakuk took it out, Havakuk lying down and Isaac paddling, trying to look nonchalant, like two guys enjoying a day on the water. Anchored near the yacht were a few fishing boats, a British merchant vessel, and HMS *Childers*, a Royal Navy destroyer engaged not long before in blocking Jewish refugee boats in the Mediterranean. The two spies got close enough to the *Grille* to make out a few figures on board and to decide their appearance wasn't Arab. They thought the figures were German.

When the pair got back to the rooftop room, Havakuk radioed all of this over the clothesline.

EVEN AS PREPARATIONS moved ahead, Isaac remembered thinking the attack would be aborted in the end because of one of the prime complications for the Beirut cell—the presence in the same city of ordinary Jews. The small community in Lebanon's capital, mostly Syrian Jews linked by blood to the nearby communities in Aleppo and Damascus, had long benefited from the tolerant heterogeneity of Beirut, from the influence of the French, and from the cosmopolitan breezes of the Levantine coast. But the Jews' position was eroding here, as it was everywhere in the Arab world. War hysteria now made their loyalties suspect, no matter how much distance they tried to put between themselves and the Zionists, no matter how abject their declarations of fealty to the Arab cause. Those declarations rang hollow, as in most cases they were. The local Jews were hostages, and they were saying whatever they needed to say to keep themselves safe. They'd become the targets of "wild behavior," Gamliel wrote in one report, with several bombs thrown in their Beirut neighborhood. Any Israeli attack here could implicate the local Jews and endanger them further.

Several acts of sabotage proposed by the spies were scrapped to avoid reprisals, and the cell had orders to avoid all contact, in keeping with an old Arab Section rule that sought to draw a clear line between Jewish agents and Jewish residents. The Palmach officer Yigal Allon, one of the Section's founders, discussed the question with other Zionist leaders in 1944 and made the point in exaggerated fashion: "Once," he said, "an envoy of ours in an Arab country asked me what he should do if he's walking in the street and sees Arabs beating a local Jew." Should the agent ignore it? Should he intervene? "I told him, join the attackers," Allon said.

The rule was wise, and was later broken with disastrous consequences. "The Affair," as the fiasco became known in Israel, began in 1951 with the idea of organizing Egyptian Jews for the purposes of "distributing propaganda" and evolved into using them as saboteurs. The cell was blown, its members jailed or executed. One committed suicide in prison. The operation, and the question of who approved it, would become one of the young state's worst political scandals.

The question of contact with local Jews seems to have arisen often for our spies in Beirut, and was discussed in more than one transmission from headquarters:

> You understand of course that we cannot change our operational principles regarding contact with Jews. It is possible that we lose some things, but in the long term we guarantee more important things.

The "more important things" were the lives of the native Jews of the Arab world. Now we take for granted that Jews had no future at all in the Arab world, but that wasn't obvious right away. In Isaac's hometown of Aleppo, for example, the Jews had survived the destruction of the Temple in Jerusalem by Rome in 70 CE, the birth of Christianity, the Byzantine Empire, the birth of Islam and the Arab conquest, dynasties of Arabs, Turks, and Mongols, and at least one devastating earthquake that destroyed much of the city. Why wouldn't it survive the birth of the State of Israel? The complete eradication of Jews in Aleppo, or in the rest of the Arab world, didn't seem possible. It seemed more likely that this too would pass. So it was wise for the agents to observe the line, and for the Jews of Beirut to remain off limits.

But the line was never clear and couldn't have been. People like Isaac and Gamliel may have believed that when operating in Beirut they weren't local Jews—that they'd transformed themselves since leaving Aleppo and Damascus and were now people called Israelis. But they hadn't been away for very long, and in Arab eyes they couldn't really have been distinguishable from Syrian Jews who'd never left, or from the Syrian Jews who made up most of the community in Beirut. In the Arab world the difference between "Israelis" and "Jews" never caught on; then and now, they're all generally called Jews. The more agents who were caught—Iraqis, Syrians, natives of the Arab world—the worse the confusion became.

In accounts of the Arab Section written long afterward, the men are generally described as Israeli spies, and tend to describe themselves that way too. But when they left for their mission in early 1948, there was no Israel, and the term *Israeli* had never been used. What they really were at the time is blurrier, and this blurriness explains some of the actions that would seem, to a professional spy service, to be reckless violations of basic precautions. While undercover in Beirut, for example, Gamliel arranged for his parents, who still lived in the Damascus Jewish Quarter, to come and meet him. His condition, he wrote later in his own defense, was that they "not ask me unnecessary questions." It was just that he hadn't seen them in years and he missed them. It would be the last time he saw his father, who died not long afterward. The three of them sat in a café by the seaside promenade, two native Syrian Jews and their son, the Israeli spy.

Following the order to avoid the Beirut Jews was especially painful for Gamliel, because two of his brothers lived in the city. He admitted later to occasionally meeting his brother Khalil (known in Hebrew as Abraham), who worked as an underwear salesman. Gamliel says he went over to Khalil's house only after his children were asleep and after swearing him to secrecy. He also saw the other brother, Subhi (known in Hebrew as Matzliakh), who sold pharmaceuticals. Of the three brothers, only Gamliel was a spy. But as Jews, they all had complicated identities and more than one name. Whether selling underwear or collecting intelligence, they were all carefully navigating the increasingly perilous Arab environment into which they'd been born.

One of the first things Isaac did after he arrived in Beirut was to take an unauthorized trip home to Aleppo, crossing the Lebanon-Syria border with his Palestinian papers. Havakuk went with him. Isaac justified the risk by saying they'd look out for military preparations in Syria, but he doesn't seem to have believed this himself. He just needed to go home for a few hours, to reassure himself that he came from somewhere, that his earlier incarnation, Zaki Shasho, was a real person. Many immigrants can identify with the impulse. It had been six years since he'd run away to join the Zionist pioneers without telling his father.

The two agents walked through the maze of alleys toward the quarter where the Jews had always lived, not far from the great Citadel that dominated the bazaar streets. Isaac's father had died since he left, and his mother had been dead since he was a child, but he believed his stepmother was still alive and living in the Jewish

Quarter. When he found her courtyard, she wasn't there, and someone said she'd moved. Many Jews had already escaped the city by that time, their rooms now occupied by strangers. After the United Nations vote to partition Palestine the previous fall, Arab rioters burned hundreds of Jewish homes and stores and nearly all of the synagogues. It wasn't like the old days, when this was their own little world. You had to be careful whom you met and what you said.

When Isaac finally found his stepmother in a different courtyard, and when she came out and saw him, she recited incantations against jinn and the evil eye—she'd thought he might be dead, and when she saw him she still thought he might be dead. She led him into her simple room and fed him his favorite food, bread balls and white cheese.

We were sitting in Isaac's kitchen as he told this story, my digital recorder between us on the table, and every so often he'd laugh or grin at one of the details, which was usual for him. But when he described this food to me, he closed his eyes for a moment and his smile was broader than I'd ever seen. He could still taste it.

That was the last time he saw his city. Before leaving he asked his stepmother to say nothing, but word spread anyway. Another man I know from Aleppo remembered the rumor passed among the Jewish kids for whom Isaac was a hero—Zaki Shasho, the janitor's son, who'd vanished one day and was somewhere in the Land of Israel fighting the Arabs instead of living at their mercy. No one had seen him in years, but now it was said he'd been glimpsed one day that summer, moving in the alleys like a ghost.

Each of the agents experienced moments of acute longing for his own people. Gamliel, in his recollections, mentions one such moment from several years later, when he was planted in Europe as an Arab journalist. One night he passed a synagogue on a Jewish festival and stopped some distance away to watch. He saw worshippers going in and out. Faint passages of Hebrew prayers drifted out and reached his ears, the supplications of Gamliel's father and grandfather: *Compassionate and merciful . . . forgive us . . .* He nearly broke down. "But that's not me," he reminded himself. He was an Arab Muslim named Yussef el-Hamed. He kept walking.

For Yakuba the moment was in the spring of 1948, when he'd crossed into Syria on foot with another agent to look at army positions. In Arab dress, with daggers in their belts, they made it to Damascus. It was a Friday.

The agents decided to do some sightseeing and went to the famous Damascus souk. In one of the stalls, Yakuba found a miniature set of copper dishes with a jug, little cups for coffee, and a dish for sugar. Yakuba bought one set and asked the Arab seller if he had another. Not in the shop, the man said, but he had one at home, and he invited the two Palestinian Arab visitors to accompany him.

On the way, the man asked them what was happening in Palestine. The 1948 war was a few months old at the time, and Arab prospects looked good.

You'll see, by God, we'll slaughter all the Jews, Yakuba replied, pointing to his dagger. With your help we'll slaughter them in three days, no problem.

The merchant didn't respond as expected. "He was quiet as he walked," Yakuba recalled, "and seemed withdrawn. We thought he must be a simpleton." The three of them navigated the alleys and arrived at the merchant's home, and when the gate to the courtyard opened, Yakuba understood right away. It was Friday evening and he smelled Sabbath food.

We have a problem, Yakuba whispered to the second agent, who wasn't sure what Yakuba meant.

I think he's *one of our people*, Yakuba whispered, indicating the smell.

What are you talking about? the second agent said. That's just Syrian food.

The merchant left them sitting in the living room as he went to look for the dishes. Yakuba was sure the man was a Jew. He knew the smell. He looked around the room. He looked up. Above his head was an elaborate copper light fixture. On it was a word engraved in Hebrew letters: *Zion*.

"We both turned pale and choked up," Yakuba remembered. Speaking as his Arab alter ego, Jamil, he'd just bragged that they were going to slaughter the Jews. When the man came back, Yakuba only barely managed to keep from blurting out the truth. He wanted to say, "We're your brothers, the Children of Israel. Be strong and brave." The Jews were a small local tribe. Their affinity for each other was deep, as was their sense that their fate in the Middle East was precarious and linked. But the two agents said nothing. They just paid for the dishes and left.

Yakuba recounted this story many years later, after a long intelligence career, to a researcher collecting oral testimonies. At this point in the transcript, the interviewer inserted a note: "He can't go on speaking."

The officers at Arab Section headquarters did their best to maintain the separation between their agents and Jewish residents, believing they could protect the Beirut community from accusations of double loyalty. The *Grille* strike, which would take place at the harbor, would look like the work of an outsider coming from the sea. The operation was cleared to proceed.

16: The Saboteur

November 24, 6:00 a.m.
Gamliel from The Dawn:
The password on the beach when the boat arrives will be
as follows:
Isaac will ask: *Min hada?* [Who's there?]
The man who gets out of the boat will say, *Ibrahim.*
Isaac will ask: *Hal aja kaman Mustafa?* [Is Mustafa with
you?]
Be strong!

The first anniversary of the UN partition resolution was
approaching on November 29, also marking a year since the
beginning of the Independence War. The date added symbolism
to the job at hand:

November 29, 6:15 a.m.
Gamliel from The Dawn:
The mission will be carried out today, Monday, the twenty-
ninth (29) of November, the anniversary of the United
Nations declaration.

The saboteur clambered out of the dinghy onto the beach just
after 9:00 p.m. Rika wore a wet suit under civilian clothes and

carried a suitcase with flippers, two limpet mines, a bottle of rum to warm him up when he came out of the water, and "energy pills," probably methamphetamines. His trainer, a veteran of the Palmach's naval unit, thought these were particularly important; once, when the Jews were retaliating for the British refugee blockade, he'd been caught after tiring in a rough sea during an attempt to bomb HMT *Ocean Vigour* in Cyprus.

If the Beirut agents weren't waiting for Rika on the beach, his instructions were to head for the backup point at the Casino Méditerranée, and if they weren't there, he was to spend the night at Chez Madeleine, one of the brothels in the red-light district off the Place des Martyrs. But this time it went smoothly. Isaac conducted the exchange of passwords, then walked Rika over to the Oldsmobile, where Yakuba was waiting in the driver's seat.

When they got close to the harbor they pulled onto the roadside, and though a few cars passed and lights were on in a nearby store, no one seemed to look at them twice. Isaac helped the saboteur open the trunk, and they were removing the mines from the suitcase when something exploded. They spent a moment looking at the rum bottle shattered on the ground. It's safe to assume both were more nervous than either let on afterward.

Rika then discovered a more serious problem: one of the limpet mines had a defective detonator. There was nothing he could do about it now but hope the second mine triggered the first. With both mines strapped to his waist, Rika crossed the sand and slipped into the water.

Hitler's yacht was illuminated, and Rika was worried there was too much light—he'd be spotted, a moving black shape visible against the ripples glimmering on the surface of the harbor.

He saw that the bow faced the beach, which wasn't the way the ship was positioned in the aerial photo, and changed his course accordingly. A second vessel towered over the *Grille*, and this was the source of the projectors lighting up the water and the Nazi yacht—the British warship *Childers*. Rika tried to get as close to the *Grille* as he could while avoiding the light, but then he saw silhouettes on board and heard voices, so he dove. He broke the surface only to see a blocky shape approaching quickly above the waterline and froze as a fishing boat passed right by him. One of the fishermen was standing on deck, another sitting. They didn't notice the swimmer treading water a few yards away.

When they'd passed, Rika struck out for one end of the *Grille*, reached the hull, and swam along its length. Now the vertical curve of the ship concealed him from the people on deck. He attached the defective mine, swam a short distance, attached the good one, and set the detonator: "The ampoule slipped the whole time, until I stopped it with one hand and broke it with another," as he described it. "After that I removed the safety catch and swam away from the ship." He moved as quickly as he could, reducing the distance to the shore, praying for the mines not to go off with him still in the water.

A GIDDY RADIO message from headquarters came down the clothesline on the rooftop and clicked into the radio receiver a day later, after Rika was extracted from the beach and returned to Israel:

Congratulations are sent to you from all those who participated in the operation. You demonstrated a first-rate ability to execute—here's to more success.

[Rika] made it safely back to base. He's full of admiration for your confidence, and hasn't stopped telling us great things about all of you, which makes us all happy and imparts a feeling of trust and appreciation. . . . All members and commanders of The Dawn are in awe of your conduct— be strong and succeed always.

The men in Beirut may not have wanted to spoil things, but they weren't sure any congratulations were due. When the sun rose, Hitler's yacht was bobbing peacefully at anchor, mocking them, two harmless Jewish mines invisible below the waterline.

It was the same the next morning, and the next.

The spies heard they were to make another attempt within a few days, but then it was pushed off by a few more days, then postponed again. Two weeks passed. Hope had been conclusively abandoned when a deep thud came from the harbor.

The explosion, when it finally happened, "caused a flame 30 meters high," according to a dramatic report in one of the Beirut papers. The mine was attached to the fuel tank in the bow, the report said, and left a hole the size of a large dining room table.

Water entered the ship and there were fears she could sink, but the German sailors and engineers managed to block the water and save her. Investigators believe it was a magnetic mine with at least 25 kilograms of explosives, attached to the ship 1.5 meters below water level. The damage is estimated at 100,000 pounds.

A few theories circulated in Beirut about the mysterious blast. One said the mine was leftover ordnance from the world war that floated in by chance from the Mediterranean. Another credited a gang of local criminals called the Black Hand, enemies of the family of the *Grille*'s wealthy Lebanese owner. There was a version crediting "anti-Farouk" terrorists—that is, an Arab nationalist faction opposed to the Egyptian monarch, for whom the yacht was intended. No one seems to have even considered the Jews.

If the Israelis were insulted, they didn't show it. There were more celebrations at headquarters, and the operation was recorded as a great success. The *Aviso Grille* was repaired but never refitted as a warship and never taken to Egypt. The ship was sold at a loss by its owner and sailed across the Atlantic to the Delaware River, where it was broken up for scrap. The toilet from Hitler's suite was salvaged and sat for many years in an auto shop in Florence, New Jersey.

There's a whole chapter dedicated to the *Aviso Grille* operation in the Israeli navy's official history of the 1948 war, though for reasons of pride or secrecy, the account leaves out the role of the spies, and the navy takes all the credit. The teacher Sam'an, known for modesty and understatement, called the strike "a classic model for any complex operation."

One would like the classic model to end with a blast lighting up the harbor, vaporizing the ship, and sending Nazis flying into the water as the saboteurs quietly clink glasses at a window nearby. One would like the course of a naval battle altered at the last moment. Instead we have the expenditure of great effort and bravery based on information that was murky and possibly misunderstood, driven by motivations not always what they seemed, tripped by technical glitches, all for an effect impossible to predict beforehand and hard to measure afterward. For a true spy story, this may indeed be the classic model.

17: The Gallows

If you attach a cone to the wall of a room, it will cause the death or severe injury of anyone in the room.

If you attach a cone to a tank of benzene made of concrete or metal, it will blow up the tank.

If you attach a cone to a car it will kill all passengers.

In keeping with the above, prepare a plan for appropriate targets and update me.

This was transmitted from headquarters to Yakuba five days after the *Grille* operation. Yakuba had been sent to Beirut with instructions to wreak havoc, and he came not only with weapons but with his explosive personality. This was a war, and he was here to bring the fight to the Arabs as the Arabs had brought the fight to the Jews.

Yakuba's attention now became focused on the great refinery at Tripoli, in northern Lebanon. He dreamed of raising it in the air like the Middle East's most spectacular firework. Isaac joined one of his scouting missions to the installation, and they drove together up the coastal road in the Oldsmobile taxi, Jamil and Abdul Karim, just as they'd driven a different Oldsmobile through Haifa after blowing up the garage eight months before.

Security at the refinery turned out to be scant. The pair of spies wanted to know what was kept in the different tanks—benzene, diesel, crude—so Isaac just climbed atop one of them with a tin can tied to a string and weighted with a stone, and low-ered it down. The plan was to cut through a fence and attach three cone bombs to one of the tanks and a fourth to a nearby aqueduct. The first tank would ignite the others, and the flammable liquids would flow downhill toward the beach and immolate the refin-ery itself. This target wasn't a new one. The first significant act of Jewish-British cooperation in Palestine during the shared panic of 1941 had been a mission to sabotage the same refinery, then under Vichy control: The open boat *Sea Lion*, carrying twenty-three Jewish fighters and a British observer, set out and was lost at sea with everyone aboard. By 1948 the men of the Special Operations Executive were safely back in Britain, writing novels and teaching ancient Greek, but Yakuba's plan was their kind of plan.

It was around this time that the feud began between Yakuba and Gamliel. It hadn't ended fifty years later, when Yakuba taped his rec-ollections, preserving his opinion of the other man for posterity, and when Gamliel published his account of those years and did the same.

Gamliel saw himself not only as the agent in charge but as the sole responsible adult. Yakuba thought Gamliel was a prig, if not a coward. Both understood their job as saving the fragile Jewish state, but Gamliel thought this meant understanding the Arab world that was trying to destroy it, while Yakuba thought it meant opening a new front. The clash had less to do with tactics than with personality. Yakuba was fiery and resistant to discipline. Gamliel seems to have been rational and even-tempered much of the time, though he wasn't entirely consistent. In his recollections he admits that while in Beirut he consulted with a coffee reader and an Armenian fortune teller, crediting them both with genu-ine insights into the future. And it wasn't that he never proposed attacks; in an earlier chapter we've seen a list of potential targets that he passed on to headquarters, and he once suggested blowing up the food warehouses at the Beirut port to make the Lebanese rethink their participation in the war against Israel. But he leaned away from actions like that. Gamliel was so averse to bloodshed, as you'll remember, that he'd once made the Section commanders promise he'd never have to kill anyone.

Instead he undertook projects like becoming a member of the Syrian Social National Party, a popular faction with fascist leanings, so he could provide informed analysis of an important player in Lebanese politics. Under his alias Yussef el-Hamed, Gamliel acquired an SSNP membership card and became deputy head of a neighborhood party branch, attending meetings and exchanging straight-armed salutes with other members. He submitted reports on speeches by the party leader and sent photographs he snapped at rallies, like this one from March 1949:

That's what he thought a spy did. He opposed his rival's fixation on destroying the refinery.

The intellectual approach wasn't one the other agent respected. Gamliel, said Yakuba, "thought his job was to get up in the morning and read the paper." Yakuba, on the other hand, knew he had a reputation as a wild man, and admitted it: "I was a wild man." Headquarters wasn't sure about his plans for the refinery, and one message from Israel warned him not to dare do anything without permission. The commanders were worried he'd go ahead even without orders.

Buried in his recollections, we find that the volatile agent had a second preoccupation in those same months. The Lebanese authorities held public executions at dawn in downtown Beirut, and he used to go to watch. The gallows were simple. The deed would be done by removing a plank from beneath the feet of the condemned, and when that happened, people clapped. You could get within a few yards. The prisoner ascended the gallows in a hood but would sometimes ask to have it removed, and you could see his face. Some of the condemned wet themselves or babbled incoherently. Some cried, and others would shout, cursing the police and the government. One criminal particularly impressed Yakuba, a robber and murderer who was said to have stuffed dismembered victims in coal sacks. Yakuba watched as this man declined a hood and addressed the crowd. I'm a murderer? the man shouted. The biggest murderer is the corrupt government that tortures, starves, executes, and abuses the people!

Then he turned to address the executioner: When you hang me, you're only doing your job, and I must give you a kiss. He kissed the hangman. Yakuba couldn't forget that afterward, how he kissed him, and then the hangman pulled the plank and the man dangled.

The agent didn't attend executions because he enjoyed them. He did it because Yakuba, who of the four spies was most prepared to inflict death, was the most prepared to face it. He thought one day it would be him standing there, and he wanted to know how it would feel. Much of the Arab Section was already dead. What would Yakuba do when his turn came? "There was a time," he remembered, "when I thought I'd shout as loud as I could, in Hebrew, 'Long live the State of Israel!' But then I came to my senses and said, no, that way I'll get the rest of the network caught and incriminate everyone else. So I'll keep quiet and they'll bury me like a dog."

THE RELUCTANCE AT headquarters to let Yakuba loose in Lebanon is explained, at least in part, by the shift in the course of the war since the terrible early days of the year. The offensive of the Arab states had been blunted by the Jew's ferocious defense and by the Arabs' own disorganization and rivalries. The mood in the Arab armies had changed. Early on, there had been much confident talk of throwing the Jews into the sea, but there was little of that now. The current frame of mind was apparent in some war talk Gamliel picked up about the Lebanon-Israel border, where Lebanese army units were serving alongside Muslim volunteers from Yugoslavia:

I heard from a Syrian soldier who spoke of the attack on Malkiya, about the weakness of the Lebanese and Yugoslav forces, and about the rapid Hagana attacks. He says the Hagana man always appears suddenly, in the sweetest hours of sleep.

Jewish forces no longer just held out, but held the upper hand. Until now the Jewish state had seemed obscured in fog, its lines dim and shifting, but now it began to solidify. It was going to be a real place.

One of the new Israeli government's first moves was to get rid of all the old partisan militias that existed before the state. That meant not just militant rightist factions, which had operated outside the mainstream leadership, but also the Palmach itself, the heart of the Jewish military underground, and the force to which the Arab Section had always belonged. The Palmach represented the left wing of the kibbutz movement, people for whom social-ism and world revolution weren't a pose; photos of Stalin were displayed in some kibbutz dining halls well into the 1950s. The Palmach's subversive attitude to government was useful as long as the government was British, but now the government was Jewish, and too fragile to risk leaving such threats intact. So although Palmach units were still fighting throughout that summer and fall, the country's leaders had already begun dismantling the militia's separate headquarters and would eventually disband the Palmach altogether.

The changes afoot weren't only military. The old Land of Israel, with its eucalyptus trees and modest shacks, its chaotic intensity and many contradictions, its multitude of possible futures and room for unlikely and irresponsible ideas—this place had to be tamed to allow a real country to emerge. The new state was going to be larger than the dream, because it was real. And it would be smaller than the dream, because it was real. Much had to be dis-carded, including the Palmach. So powerful was that little world, with its unforgettable camaraderie—"love sanctified with blood," in the words of one of their songs—that many of the fighters never got over it. Having maneuvered their rickety life raft against steep odds to an actual rescue ship, they found they missed the raft. At home in the Land of Israel, they never got used to the state of that name. The famous Palmach officer Yigal Allon, for example, went on to become an Israeli general and a prominent politician. He's still remembered as a national hero. But after he died, another fighter from 1948 eulogized him as follows: "Yigal Allon died without a homeland. The state he created robbed him of his homeland."

The Palmach posed a problem for the new government and army, but the value of its Arab Section was clear. The people now in charge took intelligence seriously. The days when the spies improvised their own cover stories and lacked money for bus fare were over. On September 16, 1948, the intelligence director Big Isser wrote a memo declaring that the Arab Section, formerly of the Palmach, was changing hands. It would now be a unit of the Israel Defense Forces. The name would be Shin Mem 18—*shin* and *mem* being the Hebrew initials of *sherut modi'in*, or "intelligence service." The unit now had an office with a desk, a clerk, and a budget. There was a recruiting officer who had access to the ID cards of new army draftees, and who passed along every Mizrahi name he found. As time went on, the teacher Sam'an took on more responsibilities in the new intelligence apparatus, which meant he was less involved with the Section he'd created and with the men he'd recruited and trained, who saw him as their father.

These changes were mostly invisible to the agents in an enemy capital to the north, working at the Three Moons kiosk, driving their taxi, sending messages through their clothesline. Their only connection to home was clicks on the radio. They had no idea who was on the other end, and assumed it was still the same people they knew. Gamliel, Isaac, and Havakuk had been dispatched before the declaration of independence in the spring, so they'd never been in the "State of Israel." In message traffic they still called it the Land of Israel. They'd never met anyone from the Israel Defense Forces, to which they supposedly belonged. When they looked out from the rooftop room, nothing had changed. In one direction was the sea. In all others, stretching to the horizon, was the Arab world.

As 1948 became 1949 in Beirut, Gamliel and Yakuba vied to lead the team after the *Grille* bombing—one toward intelligence gathering and analysis, the other toward sabotage. The Palmach's Arab Section might now be a military unit, but the idea of a proper hierarchy was foreign, and no one at headquarters seems to have been able to impose one on the men in the field. The message traffic includes attempts to sort out their bickering and decide who must obey whom, like this transmission addressed to Gamliel:

> Yakuba has every authority to plan and prepare military operations, but must consult with you regarding their planning and preparation. And every operation approved by us must be agreed upon by both of you.

That didn't help, and it was never settled. Isaac and Havakuk watched from the sidelines, evoking one of the Arabic sayings Isaac used to collect on the street:

> *Iza ana amir wa-inta amir—min rah yisuq el-hamir?*
> If I'm a prince and you're a prince—who'll drive the donkeys?

Isaac and Havakuk weren't princes. They seemed happy to drive the donkeys. In any case, the spies were never allowed to blow up the refinery. It's possible the commanders didn't want to antagonize the Lebanese unnecessarily, and there's a suggestion in one source that they were reluctant to anger European companies with financial interests in the installation. The Israelis were concerned, as always, about endangering the local Jews. There were many reasons to abort, and cooler heads prevailed.

Yakuba railed against the decision and seethed at the feeble minds at headquarters, not for months, but for years. When the surviving men got together four decades later, in their sixties, he still hadn't let it go. "If they'd accepted our plan when we were there," he insisted, according to a transcript of the 1985 meeting, "we could have cut off the fuel supplies of the Syrian and Jordanian armies and it would have entered the history books."

When Gamliel recorded his memories five decades after the events, he was angry too. "When he talks about the period in Lebanon," Gamliel said of his nemesis, "as if he, or we, or others, could have worked miracles, blowing up mountains and carrying out sabotage that would have shocked the world, it's not just fantasy—I don't want to say 'evil.'" Parts of Gamliel's book on the Arab Section are dedicated to hashing out his feud with the other agent; by this time both of them were around eighty.

18: The Jewish State

In the circles of students and intellectuals it is known that many of their friends who were officers in the Syrian army have been killed in combat with the Jews.

The regular man on the street has no idea what is happening on the various fronts. . . . Everyone knows the Jewish force is vast and there is no way to face it on the battlefield.

That message came from Damascus, where the agent Shimon, the one who'd smuggled in the radio, had moved to open the Arab Section's second foreign station. By early 1949 the fighting in Palestine was finally winding down and armistice talks were under way. It was the moment that the Hebrew poet Nathan Alterman, writing early in the war, imagined would be like a kind of grim sunset:

> And the land will grow quiet, and the sky's red eye
> Will fade slowly over smoking borders.

But the land wasn't going to grow quiet so quickly. At first the Jews thought the fighting would be followed by peace, and then by the normalization of the newly independent Jewish state among newly independent Arab states like Syria, Jordan, Lebanon, and

Iraq. Millions of people had just been displaced across Europe and were moving on, so why wouldn't that happen in the Middle East too? "At the time I thought the war was over," the writer and Palmach veteran Yoram Kaniuk writes of those days in his memoir *1948*. "I thought the Arabs would finally come to terms with us, and we with them, and we would live in our state, next to a Jordanian state or some other state, for many years."

But people watching the Arab world beyond the smoking borders, including our spies, knew that few saw it that way. Nor did the spies, who were native to the Arab world, expect it to be seen that way: Israel's unwilling neighbors were never going to accept this defeat by a minority on their own territory.

In early 1949, Radio Damascus informed listeners that a certain Jamal Nassir was heading out on a lecture tour in England "to explain that the war was lost not to Jewish arms but to American dollars and Czech planes." When the Arab Liberation Army was beaten back by a small number of defenders at Kibbutz Mishmar Ha'emek in Galilee, its commander, al-Qawuqji, publicly insisted that the fighters at the kibbutz were actually non-Jewish Russians. The humiliation was deep and wouldn't just go away.

"The Arab office in London has issued a statement saying the Arabs have not lost the war against the Jews but only the first round," said a report on Near East Arabic Radio. "The time will come when full-scale hostilities will be resumed by the Arab armies." One of the Ramallah newspapers called for compulsory military training of Arab youth so the "battle could be resumed and the Jews routed." If the Jews thought they'd won, "they are the victims of their own lying propaganda," the announcer Azmi Nashashibi said on Jordan's Radio Ramallah. "The truth of the matter is that the Arab politicians have lost the first round of the struggle but the Arab armies have not been defeated."

In Israel the mood was different. The Israeli papers were reporting the beginning of the stubborn life that characterizes the Jewish state to this day: Emergency regulations were repealed in Tel Aviv, and cafés could now stay open to 1:00 a.m. The Assis juice factory opened a new production line extracting alcohol from orange peels. A strike at the Ata textile factory was settled in favor of the workers. The Jaffa post office, closed since the British pullout, now reopened. And immigrants poured into the country through the Haifa port, thousands every week, nearly twenty-five thousand in February alone, a quarter of a million that year. The population grew by a percentage point every ten days.

Looking carefully at those details, two important divergences are visible. The first, more obvious, is the dramatic divergence of Israel's society from the countries around it. The second is in that last detail, the boatloads of newcomers, and requires more explanation. That's the moment when the real Israel diverged from the state of its founders' imagination. There are few things more important to grasp about the country today, and it's why the story of these spies is one worth telling now.

At the beginning of this story, in the first month of 1948, nearly all the Jews in the Land were from Europe, led by the austere socialists of the Zionist movement. The State of Israel was in the Middle East, but it was dreamed up in Europe as a solution to a European problem, the chronic and pathological hatred of Jews. The other Jewish world, the one in the lands of Islam, faced less organized hostility and seemed more stable. So although Zionism had attracted some from this world, like our spies, it hadn't succeeded in moving the masses.

The few who did come to the Land might have been good for some folklore, or for intelligence work, but they weren't important, and they weren't a threat. They were an exotic detail. The Arab Section was an outlier in the Palmach, a curious feature. It had been created by Ashkenazi officers, and remained under the overall command of Ashkenazi officers, and you could safely attend a Section bonfire and enjoy the Arabic songs and coffee without having it upset your own idea about what the country was or would be.

When our spies left for their mission beyond the border, most of the Jews of Islam were still in their native communities, as they'd been for centuries—a million people in enclaves from Casablanca to Kabul. Now, from their perch at the Three Moons kiosk in Beirut, the men of the Arab Section watched this world end.

"The newspaper *Al-Nasr* reports, citing reliable sources," reads an Arab Section dispatch from early 1949, "that 80 percent of the Jews in Damascus, and their possessions, are missing from the city without permission from the authorities, and there are concerns that these Jews have been smuggled to the State of Israel." A few weeks later came the following report:

> The Jews of Damascus are concentrated in their neighborhood. They have freedom of movement only within the city. . . . The Syrian authorities have arrested the wealthy Jews and the owners of large businesses. More details are being clarified.

The spies phrased their reports in the impersonal language of intelligence, but the events were personal. At the time of the report from Damascus, for example, Gamliel's mother was there, and she was still there when Arab attackers murdered several Jews in the city, and when one of Gamliel's relatives was killed by a grenade tossed into a synagogue. After his mother fled, the regime seized her home and gave it to Arab refugees from Palestine.

Arab leaders had long been warning that the fate of the region's native Jews depended on the outcome of the war against Israel. "The lives of a million Jews in Muslim countries would be jeopardized by the establishment of a Jewish state," threatened one Egyptian representative in 1947, and the Iraqi prime minister suggested they be targeted with "severe measures." This now happened. Syrian papers reported a freeze on Jewish bank accounts and a government demand for a list of their assets. The regime restricted their movement and which professions they could practice, and before long their passports were stamped to identify them as Jews.

In Egypt, the Jews were living in "constant fear and anxiety," according to a report from the Israeli Foreign Ministry. Authorities had seized the property of wealthy families, while the poor Jewish masses had other concerns, like bombs thrown to deadly effect in their crowded quarter in downtown Cairo. There were deadly pogroms in Yemen, Libya, and Morocco. In Baghdad a Jewish businessman was charged with treason and hanged before a cheering crowd.

At one of the rallies held by the Syrian Social National Party, which Gamliel/Yussef attended as a party member, he heard a speech from the party's popular leader, Antoun Saadeh. The subject was the perfidy of the native Jews of the Arab world. These people will "never identify with the national mission," Saadeh warned the crowd, because they sympathize with Zionism, and will "betray us." When he said "us" he meant the Arabs. Saadeh was Christian, but Christians could be Arabs, according to the Arab nationalists, while it was generally agreed that the Jews of the Arab world couldn't, even though they were as native as anyone else. "They're getting richer at our expense and we must prevent this, by force if necessary," Saadeh said. Gamliel reported the content of the speech.

On the day the war broke out in Palestine, mobs rampaged through Isaac's old neighborhood in Aleppo, as he'd found when he made his brief visit home. They burned Jewish homes and stores, and thronged the alleys shouting, "Palestine is our land, and the Jews are our dogs!" One man I know, a teenager in Aleppo at the time, remembered peeking out from behind shutters as rioters made a pile of looted Hebrew books, prayer shawls, and phylacteries, and torched it. Another told me how he slipped out a window, barefoot, just as the mob crashed through the gate into the courtyard and set his family's apartment on fire.

The Jews hid in their homes, or in the homes of Muslim neighbors, and came out to the ruin of their community. Most escaped over the next few years, crossing the border into Lebanon or Turkey on the same smuggling routes familiar to the Syrian refugees of our own times. The last Jews of Aleppo were allowed out by the regime in the early 1990s, locking a synagogue that had been in continuous use for longer than any other on earth. Hundreds of other communities blinked out of existence in similar ways.

I've been in an abandoned synagogue in Cairo's Jewish Quarter, which is still called that, though there aren't any Jews left. I once visited the old quarter in Fez, Morocco, also empty of Jews, and a town in the Rif Mountains where the only trace of the Jews is a shade of blue they used to paint their houses. Just as the agents' new home was coming into being in Israel, the fate of their old homes was sealed. In their campfire song "From Beyond the River," the first voices would repeat, "Let's go forward, only forward"—optimistic words. But the truth was there was no way back.

The Jewish quarters of Sanaa, Tunis, and Baghdad began to empty, their residents pushed by the growing danger they faced among Muslims, and pulled by the old dream of redemption in the Land of Israel. Israel's covert immigration agents helped them onto ships and planes converging on the new state. The tents of the Israeli immigration camps filled up, and Yiddish was drowned out by dialects of Arabic. Soon it began to dawn on some observers that the Jews of Islam weren't going to be a splash of Oriental color on the state of Theodor Herzl's Viennese imagination. There were too many of them. The newcomers were going to alter the enterprise itself. Facing the Arabs in 1948, the Zionist leaders understood it was us or them, and their astute and ruthless decisions ensured it would be us. But they didn't understand who "us" was, or that it would end up being closer to "them" than they thought.

People trying to forge a Jewish state in the Middle East should have seen that Jews from the Middle East could be helpful. The newcomers might have been invited to serve as equal partners in the creation of this new society, but they weren't. Instead they were condescended to, and pushed to the fringes. It was one of the state's worst errors, one for which we're still paying. "Perhaps these are not the Jews we would like to see coming here," said one official as the scale of the human wave became apparent, "but we can hardly tell them not to come." The masses from the Islamic world, observed the Foreign Ministry in a directive to diplomats in February 1949, "will affect all aspects of life in the country."

Preserving Israel's cultural level required more immigrants from the West, "and not only from the backwards Levantine countries."

When the daily *Haaretz* sent a reporter, Aryeh Gelblum, to one of the camps housing Arabic-speaking newcomers from North Africa, he observed their "inability to comprehend anything intellectual" and their "savage primitive instincts." Their quality, he reported in April 1949, was "an even lower level than that of the former Palestinian Arabs." The article drew a furious response from an immigration agent who'd spent years among the Jews of North Africa, Efraim Friedman, who called the writer a mouthpiece for racial hatred. "What does Mr. Gelblum know about longing for the Messiah?" the official wrote. "Did he see women and children from desert oases, who had never seen the sea, rushing into the deep waters and risking their lives to reach a boat?" The fissure evident in this exchange never really healed.

These citizens have usually been regarded as a footnote to Israel's story. When the Israeli writer Amos Elon profiled the country in 1971 in his popular book *The Israelis: Founders and Sons*, for example, he didn't have much to say about people from the Islamic world. Everyone knew who "the Israelis" were. Israel still explains itself with stories from Europe—Herzl, the kibbutz, the Holocaust. But half the Jews in Israel have roots in the Islamic world, not Europe. Most of the rest were born here, not in Europe.

On an Israeli street you often can't tell who's a Jew and who's an Arab. In a college faculty lounge or corporate boardroom, you're still more likely to find Israelis with grandparents from Poland or Russia, and a slum is more likely to house people with grandparents from Morocco or Algeria, to the country's shame. But if the culture of Jews from Islamic lands was once marginal, it has now moved to the heart of the life of the country. Israel in this century makes sense only through a Middle Eastern lens, which is one reason that Westerners find it harder and harder to figure out. Trying to navigate today's Israel with stories about Ben-Gurion and pioneers will work only slightly better than trying to navigate today's Manhattan with stories about Thomas Jefferson and pilgrims. New stories are needed to better explain this place.

The original tenets of Zionist faith, the ones that were still strong in the time of our spies, included the communal ideal of the kibbutz, the desire for a "new Jew" free of Judaism, and the belief that eventually the Arab world would make peace with a Jewish state as the world moved toward greater amity. These were ideas from Europe, and they're dead. The last kibbutznik prime minister was voted out of office as this century began, as his peace plan collapsed in the Middle East of radical religion, black masks, and suicide bombers. After that, Israel's old elite, people shaped by the confident socialist spirit of the Palmach, receded to the margins.

In the ensuing ideological vacuum, Israel's Middle Eastern soul has come out of the basement. Israelis have been free to discover that being Jewish in this region is not, in fact, new; that half the people in the country have been doing it for centuries; and that here may lie some useful wisdom. This isn't a small shift in style but a change in the way the whole country needs to be understood, from its religion and politics to its pop music. I mention those examples in particular because the young Gamliel was sharp on all of them and left behind a few worthwhile observations.

On the kibbutz where he found himself in the 1940s, after leaving Damascus and before joining the spies, Gamliel complained that no one listened to the great Arab singers of his youth, like the Egyptian chanteuse Oum Kalthoum. It was all records from Europe. This lasted for decades: Beside some music carefully quarantined as folklore, and a hazy echo or two from those Arab Section campfire songs, Middle Eastern sounds were generally disdained by the keepers of Israeli culture and banished to grungy shops selling cassettes at the Tel Aviv bus station. In a record store you'd have a section for "Israeli music," which mostly meant Ashkenazi artists, and a separate section for "Mizrahi" or "Mediterranean" music, which was also in Hebrew and made in Israel but was not, apparently, "Israeli."

The Eastern sound never went away, though, and the players of the oud and *kanoun* resolutely plunked away in small clubs and living rooms, biding their time and picking up new influences— Greek bouzouki, Russian folk songs, flamenco, rock 'n' roll—until they crept in a few years ago and took over the mainstream charts. As I worked on this book in 2017, one of the Israeli papers published a list of the fifteen most played pop songs of the year, and the number of Ashkenazi artists was zero. Mainstream musicians two generations removed from their grandparents' languages are now singing in Arabic, Persian, and Ladino. The popular rocker Dudu Tassa released an album of songs by the al-Kuwaiti brothers, famous musicians from Iraq, one of whom was his grandfather. Gamliel didn't live long enough to hear one of the country's biggest stars, Eyal Golan, release a hit in 2015—a pop number about a woman in a tiny bathing suit—that includes a mention of Oum Kalthoum as someone the singer hears in the car on the way to the beach.

In 1944, to give another example, Gamliel wrote a letter from Kibbutz Ein Harod in which he seems to have been trying to make sense of the religious life of the commune. Or rather the irreligious life, because the kibbutzniks had no rabbis or synagogues and weren't supposed to believe in God. They saw their desire to return to the Land of Israel as a secular idea. Their Hebrew wasn't prayer but the coarse language of the field, with words for pilfering and fucking. For a kid from Damascus it must all have been hard to figure out.

When he was growing up in the Jewish Quarter, his family wasn't particularly stringent, Gamliel wrote. They believed in an eventual return to the Land of Israel, as Jews were commanded to. But like most Jews they didn't see it as a plan of action, not until things around them got so bad they had to consider it. He learned Hebrew, and the Bible, and prayed "with a pure heart." Secularism had never caught on in the Islamic world, so in Damascus you couldn't be a Jew without Judaism, just as you couldn't be a Muslim without Islam. Judaism was a permanent tribal identity that meant community and tradition. You couldn't alter tradition or abandon it, but you had considerable flexibility inside it. At home Gamliel's parents kept charity boxes for the sick, for the support of mystic rabbis, and for the Zionist movement's Jewish National Fund; it was all Judaism, as far as they were concerned, and all of it was "the basis of Zionism as it exists in the heart of nearly every Jew from Damascus."

> We didn't all quite know how to read and write, but we knew there was a God in heaven and that we must follow the path of the community. In Damascus there was a large community of Jews, and they followed the commandments, but were never fanatics. . . . Our whole life we dreamed of the day that God would collect us from all of the countries, and we would reach our land and witness the redemption.

The kibbutzniks would have seen the Syrian boy's outlook as a relic not long for the world. But his Judaism proved more resilient than their ideas allowed. It proved, in fact, more resilient than their ideas. The day of the great egalitarian experiment of the kibbutz, one of the most beautiful notions that humans have ever put into practice, has passed. Secularism has lost its old confidence. If you're looking for a fair summary of the country's religious zeitgeist now, and not just among Jews of Middle Eastern descent, you'll find it in Gamliel's words from 1944.

And for an example of how the men of the Arab Section help explain politics in today's Israel, take one of the formative political events of Gamliel's life, which he experienced before he was dispatched to Beirut, when the British were still in power and the Section was in action inside the borders of Palestine. One day an Arab nationalist leader banished by British authorities was allowed to return home to the town of Tulkarm. He arrived by train, and a young Arab man with him in the same carriage was Yussef el-Hamed—that is, Gamliel.

Like all Jewish kids in Damascus, Gamliel had been mocked by Muslims with the epithet *Yahudi*, Jew. But he'd never experienced anything like the scene at the station, where hundreds turned out to greet the train. At the front of the crowd was a man who was half-preacher, half-jester, and who led everyone in a chant: *Nahna nedbah el-yahud!* We'll slaughter the Jews! They shouted it again and again.

Gamliel was frightened by the looks on their faces, by the frenzy that seized them. They meant it. They were going to slaughter the Jews. "He had a kind of hypnotic effect on them," Gamliel wrote of the man. "He spun around and danced, and everyone was behind him, clapping their hands. He improvised rhymes about slaughtering the Jews and praising the bravery of the Arabs, and about his vision, the liberation of Palestine."

Gamliel's politics were always moderate. He didn't hate the enemy. "Hatred is between nations, not people," he said as an old man, "so when someone talks about 'the Arabs,' I always say that among them are people who are kind and good—I haven't found friendship among Jews as much as I've found among Arabs." But he was shaken by the incident at the train station, the way a fanatic could set a fever loose among the people. It made him pessimistic about any kind of resolution for the tiny Jewish population amid the Islamic majority. In the 1990s, when many Israelis believed a peace agreement with the Arab world was imminent, Gamliel suspected it was not, and wrote that what he saw at the station "affects me to this day."

> You need to think a great deal, and sometimes to put yourself in their place. It doesn't make me someone who wants peace at any price, at the risk of our security. . . . If 90 percent of the Arab population wants to live with us in peace, and work with us, and make a living for themselves and their family by working for Jews, or with Jews, or any way they want, it's enough to have 10 percent who will shoot someone here and there, kill one person here and two there, in order for evil winds to blow on both sides. . . . The control is in the hands of extremists with whom you have no common language. They live on a completely different level, I don't mean in terms of morality. They read their religion in completely different letters.

Gamliel is spelling out a suspicion of Israel's neighborhood rooted in long and unhappy experience, combined with an understanding that Jews have always been part of this neighborhood. The Jews who came to Israel from the Islamic world brought a deep distrust of that world; an appreciation of the importance of religion, which Westerners often don't understand; and the knowledge that nothing good befalls the weak. Many other Israelis might have seen this view as retrograde not too long ago, but the events of recent years in and around Israel have changed the way people think. In Gamliel's words it's possible to discern the mainstream political stance of Israelis now.

For half the Jewish population of Israel, the Middle East isn't new, and tension with a Muslim majority isn't new, just the latest iteration of a force that has shaped their families for centuries. Their location inside the region has changed, and the balance of power, but for the Jews of the Islamic world, now organized and armed as Israelis, the players are the same. Gamliel of Damascus saw the 1948 war differently than a Palmach fighter from Warsaw, even though they were on the same side. That's because Israel is more than one thing. It's a refugee camp for the Jews of Europe. And it's a minority insurrection inside the world of Islam.

Placing the Jews of the Islamic world at the center of Israel's story helps illuminate a few misunderstood aspects of the conflict here, like the intense animosity in the region toward Israelis as intruders—"Crusaders" or "colonialists." In Cairo, for example, there's a giant painted panorama celebrating the Egyptian army's crossing of the Suez Canal in the 1973 war, and Israeli soldiers you see in various abject poses, surrendering to heroic Egyptians, are blond. That's funny, because if you've ever seen real Israeli soldiers, you know that many of them look a lot like Egyptians. In fact, some of the Israeli soldiers at the Suez Canal undoubtedly were Egyptians.

This is all complicated and uncomfortable for the Arab world. It leads to questions about where the Egyptian Jews have gone, and the Iraqi Jews, and the Moroccan Jews, and why. It leads to an understanding that if the State of Israel is a problem for the Arab world, then it is to some extent a problem created by the Arab world by victimizing and finally expelling the Jews who were native to that world. It's better to play on European guilt, and to expunge your own, by calling Israelis "colonialists" and painting them as blond. As it happened, the Jews telling Israel's story have generally been happy to think of themselves as blond, because they'd just spent a few centuries in Europe being caricatured as swarthy Orientals. So in an odd confluence of interests, everyone was happy to forget that this representation has little to do with the actual country that you can see if you just stand on the street and look.

Understanding this part of the Israeli story also illuminates an important part of the internal debate here, which is often mis-read by outsiders. Some children and grandchildren of the Zionist founders from Europe don't know what to make of the Middle Eastern country that has emerged. They miss the old country, where these people and their voices were kept in the back room. The resentment is sometimes expressed as nostalgia for an old lib-eralism, or as criticism of "the right" or "the religious." But it's often a deeper discomfort: many Israelis weren't expecting this Israel.

"Sometimes imagination can play really dirty tricks with you," the French author Romain Gary wrote in *The Kites*, about a young

French peasant's longing for a woman and for France during the years of Nazi occupation. "It's true with women, with ideas, with countries—you love an idea, it seems like the most beautiful idea of all, and when it materializes, it doesn't look a thing like itself anymore, or it even becomes complete horseshit. Or you love your country so much you end up not being able to put up with it at all anymore, because it's never the right one." Many Israeli arguments that seem to be about other things are actually about that.

In the accepted story about Israel, people like our four spies came from the Islamic world and joined the story of the Jews of Europe. But what happened was much closer to the opposite. The Palmach, a brash militia animated by the revolutionary energy of mid-twentieth-century Europe, is famous as one of the country's founding myths. The Arab Section, a tiny outfit of Middle Eastern Jews cautiously traversing their own dangerous region, isn't famous. But the Palmach explains little about Israel now. The Arab Section explains a lot. The complicated identities of the men, their stories concealing other stories—here's a window into the complicated identity of this country, and into the stories beneath the stories it tells about itself.

19: Georgette

In early 1949, Isaac may have understood little about the future of Israel and the Middle East, or about his place in either as an Arabic-speaking Jew. But he did grasp that he was a young man alone in a great city. Beirut had cafés and beaches. It crackled with energy. Isaac and the others started going to dance clubs but found that at the better ones, like the Kit-Kat or the Black Elephant, the ones catering to foreigners and rich Arabs, you needed to know how to dance in pairs. The spies didn't, because among the Zionist pioneers, "salon" culture was scorned as bourgeois and only folk dancing was allowed.

In downtown Beirut they found an Armenian couple with a phonograph who taught ballroom dancing in their living room—aspiring bohemians with dreams of Paris, perhaps, or people fallen from somewhere more refined. Isaac and Havakuk signed up for classes. When there weren't enough women, they danced with each other. In any case, the upscale clubs weren't the only ones around; you could always go to the proletarian nightspots with hostesses who drank and danced with you, and provided other services if you could pay.

The photographic record preserved at the Palmach archive makes clear that the spies had time for recreation. Gamliel explored the Lebanese hill country:

And ate a banana:

Yakuba went skiing on Mount Lebanon:

And so did Isaac:

And Isaac also discovered the beach:

It was at the beach that Isaac found a volleyball net where a group of young Beirutis met for regular games. They were a mix of Muslims and Christians and they were liberal; even some of the girls wore bathing suits. That was where Isaac met Georgette, who was nineteen, maybe younger.

It's worth mentioning here that nearly all the spies have stories about women. It's not plausible for men at that age to go so long without romantic connection, even in conditions of extreme adversity. Yakuba/Jamil, for example, remembered a certain Marie, the daughter of a man he knew through the taxi business in Beirut. He agreed to become engaged to her because that was the only way her family would let them date. There were no casual relationships. They went to the movie theater together and maybe did other things too, it isn't clear—his recollections don't get too explicit. Marie's ten-year-old brother used to come with them when they went out, and Yakuba/Jamil would bribe him with pistachios or chocolate and tell him to get lost. He and Marie couldn't go too far anyway: "She was a virgin. I wasn't going to ruin her life." He went out with her for a while before breaking it off.

Gamliel/Yussef had a relationship with the sister of a Muslim business associate, a girl so religious that she came to their first meeting in a face veil. Here too the stated idea was marriage. Her family was in favor. The potential groom's family connections were shadowy, it was true, but he did have a store and some money. If things became serious, Gamliel mused, he could bring her back to Israel and she could convert to Judaism. That didn't happen, and they split up after a few months, but it's interesting to imagine a One Who Becomes Like an Arab returning to Israel with an Arab woman who becomes like a Jew.

A few years after this story, in the 1950s, the domestic security service Shin Bet planted several agents among Arabs inside Israel's borders; the Arab population that remained after independence was little understood by the new state and was seen as a potential fifth column. Several of the Ones Who Become Like Arabs in this group married local women as part of their cover. One of them, a Jew from Iraq, had a child with a Muslim woman who was unaware of his real identity, while at the same time his real wife and children lived in a Jewish town not far away. When he was extracted after years in the field, he had to abandon his Arab family. The moral line in this kind of warfare is hard to calculate: how does wrecking one woman's life, for example, stack up against saving the lives of forty people, or four? But in this case the tactic yielded little useful information and seems to have been abandoned after that. When the story was reported in 2015 on Israel's

Channel 10 TV, one of the journalists who uncovered the details called it "an affair the Shin Bet would rather forget."

At the very beginning of the Section, in the days of the British sabotage school at Haifa in 1941 and 1942, a few women were trained to accompany the men by posing as their wives. The problem of loneliness was understood, as was the fact that unmarried men draw attention in Arab society. Recruiting Mizrahi women wasn't easy, as we've already seen, because of the reluctance of Middle Eastern parents to let their daughters embark on such an adventure, but the spymasters did come up with a few. One of them, Esther Yemini, recalled later that she was taught Arabic, sabotage, and how to use a knife, and that none of these was her primary concern.

"They divided us into couples and started training us," she remembered. "One thing I was afraid of, maybe more than anything else, was how to protect my innocence when with my partner. I wasn't bothered about being killed, or captured and jailed. . . . I was bothered only by how to protect my innocence, and as far as I knew at the time, kissing made you pregnant." She and the other young women were eventually sent home without being put in the field, and the men of the Arab Section were left to deal with their need for companionship on their own.

The entanglement with Georgette was clearly a potent memory for Isaac, and I had to coax the details out of him. What did she look like? Regular, he said. When I pushed, he said she had dark hair. Was it long? Yes, long. Was she Muslim? She was Christian. Was she pretty? Pretty, he said. Her family was poor and her brother sold fish in one of the markets. Georgette was a girl from the wrong side of an Arab city, so the truth is they weren't that different. Isaac might not have had more in common with a socialist from Jewish Warsaw, or with the daughter of a German-speaking shopkeeper in Tel Aviv.

Isaac had use of the cell's Oldsmobile, a rare luxury for someone on Abdul Karim's rung of the social ladder. He knew it made him more desirable. After meeting Georgette for a while at the beach volleyball games, Isaac began driving her to the movies. The Beirut cinemas showed Egyptian and American films; they preferred the American ones with Clark Gable, Ingrid Bergman, and Esther Williams. They couldn't do much more than go to the movies, because Georgette couldn't bring him to meet her parents. She was Christian and Abdul Karim was Muslim, and those lines weren't crossed. But they saw each other often, and held hands. Isaac doesn't think she put on makeup, but she would wear a nice dress.

Havakuk, the watcher, had someone waiting for him at home—the Palmach fighter Mira, to whom he sent messages over the radio. The Arab Section secretary would take them to her and relay her replies. The messages are a bit stilted, as we might expect; it must have been hard to write love notes knowing they'd pass through multiple hands, be coded and rendered into Morse, broadcast to an enemy country, then recorded in a log for posterity. The ardor had to be left between the clicks of the transmitter. But Mira did her best:

15:15

To my dear Havakuk, much peace!

I received your letter with joy and great surprise. I hope you'll appear as soon as humanly possible. I'm well, working in the orange harvest while waiting for your return.

No one was waiting for Isaac, which made him more suscep-
tible to errors like Georgette. Georgette didn't think she was an
error, of course, or a threat. She didn't mean to get involved with
Israeli intelligence. She was just a young woman who was who
she said she was, and who liked the man she met at the volleyball
game. Maybe she thought she'd get into this man's Oldsmobile and
drive away from her life.

Georgette helped alleviate the fear and tedium of Isaac's work,
the lying, the tapping of the radio in the rooftop room:

> The press announces that the [Arab] League won't meet
> soon. The press also reports that the situation in Iraq is very
> tense and riots could break out at any time.

The intelligence files from 1949 show the Israelis straining
to piece together the world around them. We find hand-drawn
maps of airports in Lebanon, for example, and of the piers at Port
Said in Egypt, and sketches of Egyptian army uniforms. We learn
that the symbol of the Syrian Third Regiment is "a camel on a
red background." Isaac and the other spies in Beirut did what
they could to add detail. The big picture was the province of the
people code-named Wisdom, the intelligence collators to whom
the agents addressed their reports. No one understood much, and
even Wisdom's powers were limited, but our men knew least of
all, moving in the shadows, passing on fragments to people they
couldn't see.

Some of the material in the files seems trivial. The Beirut spies
reported the departure of the Egyptian ship *Skara*, for example,
bound for the Arabian port of Jeddah and carrying "black pepper,
various textiles, olive oil, and halva." Headquarters was interested

in ideas as well as facts, and Gamliel bought and sent two books on the rise in pan-Arab sentiment, including one by the Beirut professor Constantine Zurayk. Some of the information was of more pressing importance, like this fragment from one file:

> At the workshop of Abd el-Razek Habib, in Mahlat el-Safi, Beirut, submachine guns, grenades, and mortars are being manufactured.

In Syria, reported the Section agent in Damascus, the regime had outlawed the sale of maps for security reasons and was planning a large weapons purchase. Reports from other sources made clear the Arab states were arming. The Syrians had placed an order with Tito Bolo, an Italian arms dealer from Lugano, for one thousand English rifles, an unspecified number of 20-millimeter cannon with fifty-four thousand shells, and several Fury airplanes.

Israeli intelligence also noted that Lebanese authorities were getting between fifty and sixty emigration requests every day, many for Latin America and Europe. The Maronite Christians, the dominant sect in Lebanon, were expressing concern in the press that most of the emigrants were Christian and that this could augur "the irreversible collapse of the standing of Christians in Lebanon." Their concern was justified. In those reports, the spies were seeing an early stage of the erosion not just of Middle Eastern Christians but of all the minorities that had once been at home in the Islamic world. The Jews would go, and the Christians, and many others, leaving their home region a poorer place.

Yakuba still believed he was waging a war on enemy territory and didn't want to deal in information, however useful it was to the broader Israeli effort. A few sabotage proposals were considered. After the final defeat of the Arab Liberation Army in Palestine, for example, Yakuba discovered that the force's formerly celebrated general, al-Qawuqji, had moved to Beirut and was living quietly on the same street where Yakuba rented an apartment, by the Saint-Michel beach. This was the commander who'd once promised to "murder, wreck, and ruin" anything in Palestine that stood in the way of his victory over the Jews, but now he seemed to be at loose ends. Yakuba saw the general around the neighborhood, sometimes with his German wife, and he struck the spy as "a private guy, a good-looking guy, a lovely guy. Not arrogant." Yakuba wanted to plant a bomb in his car. But like his plan for the refinery, this too was rejected by headquarters. By the spring of 1949 the Arab general and his liberation army were spent forces. There wasn't any point.

Another proposal was to assassinate the Lebanese prime minister, Riad al-Solh. The prime minister took an aggressive line against Israel, though he was braver at the podium than on the battlefield, and Lebanon's army had contributed little in the war. The truth was that the Lebanese were less interested in things like national honor or fighting than in business and Mediterranean sunshine. This is probably why their counterespionage was so poor: a police state wasn't their style. They had the right idea, and I salute them.

The plan was to use a magnetic bomb from the weapons cache buried at the beach. Isaac was going to attach the bomb to the prime minister's car as he drove by, so the agent followed him around Beirut as he'd once followed the preacher in Haifa, hanging out at a little grocery store near the leader's home to see when he came and went. But eventually the agents were told to abort. If this were fiction, the cache at the beach would be the pistol in act 1 and would have to be used around now. But this story takes place in the real world, and the cache remained in the sand. Prime Minister al-Solh ended up being murdered two years later, in 1951, by an Arab assassin.

IN DOWNTOWN BEIRUT one night, Georgette and Isaac got into trouble when police stopped the Oldsmobile. A cop seems to have noticed that the woman passenger was sitting next to the cab driver, instead of behind him, which was irregular. An officer took down Georgette's details at the police station while a second officer questioned Isaac, who gave his name and city of origin: Abdul Karim Muhammad Sidki of Jaffa, Palestine, now displaced. The Lebanese didn't seem overly concerned with security as a matter of course, but these officers were unusually thorough, and Isaac became worried. It took a few questions specifically about his relationship with Georgette before he realized that the police suspected her of being an unlicensed prostitute working outside the red-light district off the Place des Martyrs, where licensed brothels were a source of income for the city; the authorities were determined to stamp out unsanctioned entrepreneurship. Isaac reassured the officer that they were a couple, and to make it sound better he said he might marry her one day.

This didn't make it sound better, because the policeman hated the idea of Muslims marrying Christians. That didn't happen in Lebanon, the policeman informed him, and he added a free warning: he'd better stay away from the girl, because her brother was a criminal—a "half murderer" is the way Isaac remembers it.

Isaac and Georgette resolved to be more careful after that. They wouldn't drive together anymore, just meet at the movies and walk home separately. After one of their next dates, Isaac parted from

Georgette and was heading back to the rooftop apartment when he found himself pinned against a wall in a building's dark entrance watching something glint inches from his face—it was a knife, a big one, the kind fishmongers use. "He was huge, with such a face," Isaac said when he told the story, his eyes wide in mock terror. The terror wasn't mock at the time. He knew who it was because he'd once seen Georgette's brother, the half murderer, at his stall in the market.

What's your relationship with her? the fishmonger asked, gripping Isaac in the dark. Isaac was strong but small, and no match for his opponent. He repeated what passed for the truth at the time: He was Abdul Karim, a refugee from Palestine, here without family. He and Georgette were friends.

End it now, her brother warned. You're Muslim and we're Christian, and we protect our honor. Isaac doesn't recall the exact words, but it was something to that effect.

Tell that to your sister, Isaac suggested weakly. She wants to keep going out.

End it, the man repeated, and he left Isaac panting in the dark entrance. "That's when I learned the lesson," Isaac remembered. "In Beirut it would be easier to get killed because of friction between religious sects than because you were a spy."

In our interviews, Isaac didn't want to say much more about Georgette, but the episode didn't end in the dark entrance of that building. She appears in Gamliel's account, where many details match Isaac's version: she was Christian, her brother sold fish and was an "underworld figure," and she used to drive with Isaac in the taxi. But Gamliel's description is less charitable. He says Georgette limped. "She fell in love with him," he wrote, "and asked him to marry her." Gamliel believed that their connection was genuine, and in his account, the relationship didn't end with the brother's intervention. In fact, it never really ended until Isaac disappeared.

A brief jump one year ahead, to the spring of 1950, will allow us to complete this story. When Isaac vanished one day, Georgette was furious and hurt, and even more surprised to find her absent boyfriend's Oldsmobile with a new driver—another young refugee from Palestine who had no family. She became suspicious, though it's not clear precisely what she suspected.

This new refugee was an Arab Section agent who was using the same car as his predecessor, a breach of basic precautions. His name was Yehoshua Mizrahi. When I found him at eighty-six, living in a quiet suburb north of Tel Aviv, he said the entanglement with Georgette endangered the entire Beirut operation. The message log seems to bear this out, particularly the following transmission sent from Beirut to headquarters on April 25, 1950, after Isaac disappeared:

> Our situation is dire. Isaac Shoshan's girl followed us, accompanied by ten hooligans. She asked for our names and address. We immediately changed apartments, and are trying to see each other as little as possible. She won't take her eyes off the car, and is pushing me to tell her where Isaac is. . . . We believe it's necessary for Isaac to return immediately and without hesitation, before the matter becomes known to the police, because then our situation will be most grave.

Headquarters tried to reassure the men in the field. If asked, they were to say they don't know her boyfriend, Abdul Karim—they just picked up the car secondhand from someone leaving town. But Georgette proved impossible to shake. With the network at risk, Gamliel went to meet her at a café. Georgette knew him as Yussef, another refugee connected to her vanished boyfriend. She was furious.

You don't know how much it hurts me that he lied to me—he's a liar, a betrayer, she told Gamliel/Yussef, as he recalled the conversation later. I feel, she said, like a piece of fate thrown into a frying pan on the fire.

Gamliel tried to cheer her up, suggesting that if she were on fire perhaps she should have some ice cream to cool off. This made her laugh. He empathized with her anger at the missing man, but tried to convince her that the car's new owner had nothing to do with him. If he met Abdul Karim, promised Gamliel, he'd be sure to tell him how terribly Georgette had been treated. As she stood up to leave, she gave Gamliel a photograph of herself and told him it was for Abdul Karim. On the back of the photo she'd written, "To the one who ruined my life. We will yet meet to settle accounts."

Isaac told me that Gamliel's version was untrustworthy in places, and it's true that in his writing Gamliel seems eager to portray himself as the most capable agent and to play up the mistakes of the others. From a distance of seventy years it's hard to know exactly what happened. But the outline of the story seems clear. When you're away for a long time, your real life begins to fade, and Isaac didn't even have a real life yet. It wasn't as if he had parents waiting for him in a childhood home, or a wife, or familiar neighbors. He'd lost his old country and hadn't seen his new one. He was twenty-four. It had been a year of death and isolation. Georgette was someone soft whom he could touch. She had nothing to do with the war. She was human.

This story reminds me of a documentary I saw a few years ago about a man from Nazareth, an Arab Christian named Yussef Shufani. In the 1920s, he'd been found as an infant on the steps of a Haifa church and adopted. For many years he tried to discover his origins but never did. After he died, an elderly man with many children, his Arab granddaughter discovered that her grandfather was the illegitimate son of one of the Belkind brothers, famous Jewish pioneers and fighters. There was an affair between a man and a woman, this child was born, and he became Arab. People live close to each other. Things get tangled up.

20: The Redhead

On the Israeli side of the barbed-wire line dividing Jerusalem, in a building overlooking the Mandelbaum Gate into the Jordanian sector, the teacher Sam'an stood at a window. Below him, a crowd of Arab prisoners moved toward the crossing, away from Israel and back into the Arab world. His eyes were on two of them.

The first plan had called for three agents, but when a wife who was scared and pregnant went to the Section commanders and begged them to let her husband off, they gave in. That left two: Efraim, who was twenty, born in Baghdad and raised in Kirkuk, and Bokai, a nineteen-year-old from Damascus. Bokai stood out among the men because though he was as Arab as any of them, he had light skin and reddish hair. His first name was Yaakov. In photos he seems always to appear among friends, shirt buttoned half-way. He's the one standing on the left:

It was the beginning of May 1949, exactly a year since Isaac and Havakuk were given a gun and some money at the height of the war and sent off with little more than "good luck." In the Arab Section's new incarnation as the military intelligence unit Shin Mem 18, things were more organized. There were detailed operational plans and an officer who prepared cover stories. Two weeks before their departure, Efraim and Bokai were thrown into a prison with POWs slated to be sent back to Jordan in a prisoner exchange, part of the armistice agreements that had just ended the Independence War. Their cover identities used their real countries of origin, Iraq and Syria, as if they were foreign Arab volunteers who'd come to fight. They were roughed up by the camp guards like everyone else.

Their instructions were to travel to the Jordanian capital, Amman. Within a few days of their crossing, Gamliel was to meet them there at a rendezvous point downtown, the Café el-Urdun. Until a radio set reached them in Amman, they were to communicate through letters mailed to Gamliel in Beirut; from there, Havakuk would relay the information to headquarters over the rooftop clothesline. They could also encode messages in notices submitted to the column "Letters from Refugees to Their Relatives," a regular feature in the Arabic *Al-Nasr* newspaper meant to help the hundreds of thousands of displaced Palestinians find loved ones scattered by the war. The Section, for its part, would send communiqués encoded in broadcasts on the Voice of Israel's Arabic service.

The two spies were released with a batch of prisoners on May 3 and brought to the Mandelbaum Gate. Bokai had money stashed in a Primus stove. Efraim's was in a jam jar. From his vantage point in the window above the Israeli side of the crossing, Sam'an watched them move closer to the Jordanian guards and vanish inside the little terminal building. Headquarters radioed the rooftop in Beirut: "Our two friends have crossed the border."

THE PLAN WENT wrong right away. "A report has been published in Beirut," Gamliel radioed headquarters, "of the arrest of two Jews who infiltrated into Jordan among the new refugees, and who have confessed that they came to assassinate certain individuals." Similar reports, with a few key differences, began turning up in the Hebrew papers, which seemed to be getting information from their Arabic counterparts. One paper was saying "two Arabs" caught during a POW exchange had confessed to having orders from Jews to carry out assassinations.

Were the arrested men Jews or Arabs? If they were known to be Jews, the spies were lost. If they were Arabs, it meant either that the reports referred to two different men, which seemed unlikely, or that Bokai and Efraim hadn't broken under interrogation and were sticking to their cover stories. The Section panicked. The two missing men knew there were agents in Beirut and knew both Gamliel's real name and his alias. Gamliel left immediately for Amman, missing a terse message from headquarters:

Cancel your trip and do not go to the *poste restante*. Warn your comrades against doing anything that could draw suspicion, and try to temporarily blur your footsteps to the extent possible until the facts become clear.

The Beirut agents were ordered to lie low, avoid contact with each other, hide the radio, and stay clear of their apartments. "They knew our addresses," Yakuba recalled, "and it could have toppled the whole network in a second." Another message clicked into the radio on the Beirut rooftop:

> In wake of the arrest of our two comrades in Transjordan, and the concern that they could reveal secrets during questioning, it has been decided to withdraw the two cells in Syria and Lebanon. . . . There is also concern that Gamliel could be arrested in Transjordan.[*]

Gamliel was already in Amman. But when he showed up at the café, the Jordanian police weren't waiting for him—Efraim was. The new agent was shaken and seemed ill, but managed to recount what had happened.

The POWs were told to stand in line as they waited to cross at the Mandelbaum Gate, he said. Before being allowed through, they had to file by a table where a Jordanian officer asked a few questions and gave each man a pack of cigarettes and a small sum of money before waving him past. Efraim went first, getting through without incident, and waited for his partner outside the crossing on the Jordanian side. A few minutes passed, then half an hour. The redhead never appeared. Efraim understood that his life was in danger, because if his friend was caught and tortured he'd reveal the existence of a second spy, and the Jordanians would hunt him down. Efraim was still just a few dozen yards from Israel. A few minutes earlier, everything had been fine. But this was how it happened—one slip, one second, and you were in a nightmare. There was no way back through the gate.

---

[*]   Earlier in the spring of 1949, Transjordan had officially changed its name to Jordan. But it was a while before the old name went out of use.

The only way out was forward, into enemy territory. Efraim took a bus to Amman as planned, found a hotel, and began to lose his nerve.

Afterward there was some debate in the Section about what piqued the suspicion of the Jordanian guards. Some thought it was Bokai's Syrian identity card: the Jordanians and Syrians were squabbling at the time, and the guards may have been instructed to detain Syrian nationals for further questioning. Others thought the agent's Arabic may have failed him when it counted, even though he was a native speaker; maybe he'd been living in Hebrew for too long. He was just nineteen and may have become flustered. The saboteur Rika from the *Grille* operation, who was Bokai's childhood friend from Damascus, always thought it was simply his appearance, that he didn't look like an Arab and should never have been recruited in the first place: "It's a basic error to induct a redhead into the Black Section."

Picking up the agent's trail became the Section's sole concern in those weeks. They all felt responsible for him, and they knew it could have been them—that it could still be them at any moment. Gamliel stayed in Amman, visiting the Café el-Urdun every day in case the missing man showed up. Isaac was ordered to join him and flew from Beirut to the Jordanian capital. It was his first time on an airplane.

Isaac and Gamliel scanned the Jordanian papers and listened in cafés for rumors of a Jewish spy. Nothing. They picked up some unrelated tidbits, though, and passed them on: They couldn't see much new weaponry around Jordan, and no antiaircraft batteries were in evidence. There were two Iraqi battalions in the country, but they were about to return home. It didn't look like a new round of fighting was imminent.

More important, in retrospect, were their observations of the refugees from Palestine who had flooded the desert kingdom. "I stayed in Amman for a week," Gamliel wrote afterward, "walking around the city's dusty streets, around the poor neighborhoods and refugee camps, and my heart broke at the sight of the naked children, their bellies swollen with hunger, wandering around the pathetic alleyways." The Arab Section agents weren't ideologues. They looked at other people and listened to them, and reported what they saw and heard. In those first days after the war, they were among the first to grasp what the refugees meant.

These people, Gamliel warned from Amman, weren't going to come to terms with their loss. They weren't going to move on, as the Jews had. These refugees wanted to go back to Palestine and live under Arab rule. They hated not only the Jews but the Jordanian king, Abdullah, for his perceived collusion with the Jews, or for his inability to defeat them. "They are not willing to live in barren Transjordan," Gamliel wrote, "and are convinced it would be better to die in battle than leave their homeland." In these messages from the early summer of 1949, amid the confusion over the fate of the missing spy, we see the facts, and the coming decades of conflict, begin to dawn.

Rarely did any hint of politics creep into Isaac's conversations with me. His views of the Arab world were complicated. He took its people seriously, and their culture seriously, and their hostility seriously. Like Gamliel, he had no hatred or disdain for them, and also no illusions about the fate of the weak, which is why the Jews could never be weak again. He didn't say much beyond that. The closest he ever came to a broader analysis was in the form of a parable that occurred to him when he described the refugees in

Jordan. "I think one thing our leaders have never properly understood about this region," he said by way of a prologue, "is the matter of revenge."

Once, he said, there was a Bedouin whose brother was killed by a neighboring tribe. The tribal code demanded that the Bedouin exact vengeance, but he didn't, not the next year, or the next. Twenty years went by, then thirty, and by now he was an old man, and only forty years later did he finally avenge his brother's death. After that, other members of his tribe came to him and asked, "Why did you hurry?"

AS THE SEARCH for the redhead turned up nothing, his partner left Amman and showed up in Beirut. Efraim was agitated and convinced he was being followed. He hung around the Three Moons kiosk, endangering the men, who'd resurfaced after scattering for a while and after the idea of recalling everyone to Israel had been reconsidered. They were all skittish, conscious of what the redhead might be telling interrogators at that very moment and what that could mean for them—a knock on the door in the middle of the night, arms gripping you and tearing you from bed, hard metal pressed on your temple, a dank cell, the hood and the hangman. In the end they had to bundle the frightened agent into the Oldsmobile, and Yakuba took him on a nighttime drive to a point along the Lebanon-Israel border. It was a hostile frontier but there was no fence yet, and if you timed it right to avoid the Lebanese patrols you could walk across. A few men from the Section were waiting in the darkness on the other side. Yakuba remembered the agent passing across the border back into the Jewish state, suitcase in hand, his mission a failure.

In early July, one of the Jordanian papers reported an order from King Abdullah approving the death sentence for a Jewish spy, "a soldier in the Israeli army." It sounded like Bokai, but the name in the article—Eliyahu Khader Nasser—wasn't the name the redhead used. A fake British Mandate identity card belonging to the spy, now in the Palmach archive, gives his alias as Najeeb Ibrahim Hamouda:

According to a different report, four suspected spies had been arrested, three were released, and one hanged—but the executed man was an Arab, according to the report, so the redhead might have been one of those released. Unless he hadn't broken cover and was executed as an Arab.

For Isaac and Gamliel, the most memorable moment of the search had nothing to do with the missing spy. Making no progress in Amman, they decided to travel to Jerusalem, where the agent had gone missing. The city had been divided after the fierce fighting of the previous year, with the Jews in the west and Jordan holding the eastern sector, including the Old City, so getting to East Jerusalem from Jordan's capital didn't require crossing any borders. They took a service taxi from Amman heading west down the hills of Edom, then across the Jordan River, then up into the Judean Hills. They stopped briefly at the Islamic shrine of Nebi Musa to pray with the other passengers, then continued the climb up the narrow desert highway to Al-Quds, as the Arabs called Jerusalem.

It was evening when they entered the walls of the Old City and found everything dark. The ancient streets hadn't recovered from the war, and the electricity was out. The Jewish Quarter was empty and ruined, its residents expelled, the Western Wall forbidden to the people who used to pray there.

The two agents went to a hotel that Isaac remembered from missions in Jerusalem before the war—the Petra, which stood inside the Jaffa Gate, and still does. Part of the hotel, they found, was used by a Jordanian army unit manning positions along the wall facing the Jewish sector across the armistice line. There wasn't real fighting anymore, just some sniping back and forth. Isaac introduced himself to an officer who seemed to be in charge, saying that he and his friend now lived in Lebanon and had come to see their homeland, Palestine. The officer was friendly. The hotel manager recognized Isaac from before the war, Isaac was pleased to discover, as "one of the good guys from the Jaffa jihad." The manager made sure they got a decent room.

The Jordanian officer ordered one of his soldiers to give the visitors a tour of the army posts atop the wall; traces of these emplacements are still there today, coarse cinder blocks atop the graceful Ottoman stones. Isaac and Gamliel followed their guide up the dark steps, their eyes level with the stones of the wall, then with the lip of the wall and the crenellated battlements, and then high enough to see over—and there in front of them was Jewish Jerusalem ablaze with lights.

There can't have been very many lights in the gaunt city of 1949. The fighting was barely over, and the strip of no-man's-land directly beneath them was barbed wire and rubble. But neither of them recorded the view that way. They both remembered it as dazzling.

From the Arab post, they saw the buildings of downtown Jerusalem and the Jewish traffic on Jaffa Road. This was the closest they'd come to the people they missed—the survivors from the Section and from the Palmach, their relatives, girls they thought about.

Most of Isaac's time undercover wasn't spent spying or blowing up ships. It was spent at the kiosk, selling sandwiches and erasers to schoolchildren, playing a bit part in the life of the Lebanese capital. The erasers were real. When a kid bought candy, the smile was real. Georgette was a real person. Running a little kiosk in an Arab city was a real life; it could have been his real life, had he not run away from Aleppo, had the spies not found him, had history not taken the incredible course it took in those years, carrying him along in the current. The Jewish state, on the other hand, was just clicks through a radio. Maybe it didn't exist. And if it did, maybe it wouldn't exist for long. And if it survived, maybe he wouldn't survive to see it.

And then there it was, people walking on the street, their babies crying, their poor laundry drooping and electric lights shining, Isaac's own people buying, selling, living under the guns of the Jordanian sentries along the wall, still unreachable across a hostile border but right here, right in front of him, the reason for his missing friends, for the dread in the pit of his stomach—the State of Israel.

MEANWHILE, IN THE bowels of a military prison, a nineteen-year-old wrote a letter. The prison was in Amman, not far from the desert hill called Nebo, where Moses died on the wrong side of the Jordan River, within sight of the Promised Land.

I'm looking at this letter now. Or rather at a Hebrew translation that survives; the original was in Arabic, but if it still exists somewhere I couldn't find it.

It's hard to know what to make of Bokai's letter, even after going over it many times. A modern reader might find it evoking the contradictory texts read out by hostages we've seen videotaped at gunpoint: My condition is dire, I'm being treated well, I miss you all, do what they want or I'll die. The Jordanian jailers must have known their prisoner was worth something, and they may have ordered him to write the letter hoping for an exchange of some kind—although if that's true, what happened afterward doesn't make much sense.

The captured spy seems to have befriended another prisoner, a Palestinian Arab who was about to be released. Bokai understood he wasn't likely to have another chance to get a message out and wrote a letter to his commanders, entrusting it to the second prisoner to smuggle to Israel. This, at least, was the story. It's possible, if not likely, that the spy's captors were involved in the letter's composition and dispatch.

A few aspects of the text are cryptic: the fact that Bokai, who had confessed that he was a spy, continued to use an alias; the fact that the alias he gave, the same one cited in the Jordanian newspaper report, wasn't the one in his cover story; and the fact that next to this fake name he signed the real name of his secret intelligence unit. Some parts of the letter seem distinctly Muslim. Bokai begins with the phrase "In the name of God, the merciful and compassionate," which traditionally opens Islamic texts, and goes on to convey wishes of peace to "all the believers," which is how Muslims refer to themselves. The phrase isn't common in Judaism. We aren't likely ever to know the precise circumstances in which the letter was written.

The prisoner addressed his words to the teacher Sam'an, beginning with long greetings and blessings in the high Arabic style, including "thousands of kisses and good wishes." Then he got to the point.

> If I wanted to write all that is in my heart, all the paper in the world would not be enough to express my longing for all of you, and for the homeland.
>
> Brother! I write these lines from prison in Amman, and my two hands shake from missing all of you. Know that my conscience and heart are yours, and will remain so as long as I live in this dark world.

Bokai seems to mean that he betrayed no one else. As far as anyone knows, this is true.

> I have had enough of the evil life I encounter every day, a life of suffering, mental torture, and inhuman treatment.
>
> Brother! I must inform you that the court has sentenced me to hang. I am sitting here waiting for the sentence to be carried

out. I'm sitting here in terrible conditions, bound with iron
chains that weigh more than two *rutal*.* My food is bread and
water and no more, and my eyes haven't known sleep since the
day I was caught.

There is nothing negative in my heart or thoughts, and I
still say that the mission was good, and only a few small things
caused it to go awry. I believe the man I mentioned before my
departure is the one who informed on me and led me into this
trap. And if I survive this and get back to you, we will speak
more about this, if God wills it.

Bokai seems to have warned his superiors that someone suspected him before his departure, probably another inmate at the
Israeli camp for prisoners of war. This, he thought, was who tipped
off the border guards.

Dear brother! I ask you to do everything you can to get me
out of here through the Red Cross. I am certain that you will
succeed, because such things happen here.

And now, my dear friend, I beg you to tell my friends and
relatives that I am well, and healthy, and there is no reason
to worry about me. I inquire after all our friends, and all the
commanders, and may peace be upon you and upon all the
believers.

Your faithful friend,
Khader Nasser, Shin Mem 18

---

* An Ottoman measure of weight: two *rutal* is just over thirteen pounds.

Important note: I ask you to repay the man who brings you this letter with generosity, because of the great act of mercy he has done for me.

The messenger made it to Israel with the letter and, after several delays, turned it over to the authorities. From there it made its way to the Section, arriving at the end of August and causing a stir. It was the first sign of life from the missing agent. Three weeks had passed since guards took him from his cell and hanged him.

21: Home

I t took a while longer before everyone was pulled out of Beirut. But the agent's death was the last significant episode in the life of the Arab Section.

The message log shows unmistakable signs of weariness after that. Yakuba is agitating to come home, but headquarters puts him off: replacements are being trained but aren't ready yet. Havakuk wants out too and is told the same thing. Isaac says he has an injury of some kind and wants to have it treated in Israel; he's told to seek treatment in Lebanon.

Amid routine requests from headquarters for information on the Syrian air force and on how to apply for refugee certification in Lebanon, the log contains messages from family and friends. The charming fighter Mira, now demobilized, sends Havakuk her love and loyalty—she's waiting for him. At 10:00 p.m. on September 22, 1949, Isaac is informed that his brother Avraham, who'd also made it to Israel, was just married. This made things worse. It was one thing to suffer during a war, but the fighting was over for now and life was happening in Israel, the furious kind lived by people just spared death. It was happening without them. They weren't professional spies. They weren't prepared for the long haul, or for the life of peril and boredom that is the spy's lot most of the time. And of course there was the death of the redhead, which forced them to face the risk they were running.

Before following the men home, there's one last story from Beirut worth telling.

Next to the spies' kiosk, on the street by the Three Moons, was a little shop where an Armenian fixed watches. Another store was owned by a shoemaker, and in a third was a man who patched flat tires. The tire fixer used to come over to chat when business was slow. He knew the men in the kiosk were refugees from Palestine, and he liked to bring them news. If he had customers who turned out to be Palestinian, he'd sometimes escort them over to meet Abdul Karim, Ibrahim, and the others.

One day, Isaac remembered, the tire fixer showed up at the kiosk with a man in a simple suit. This man looked old, maybe seventy, though the events of those years bent younger people and slowed their movements. As always, Isaac/Abdul Karim made sure to ask the man where he was from before he could be asked himself. When the man said Haifa, Isaac said he was from Jaffa. The tire fixer went back to his shop, leaving the refugees alone.

The man told Isaac his story. He fled Haifa when everyone fled, the man said. Now he lived in a refugee camp. But he hadn't got to the point yet. There was something else.

The old man had two sons. They were mechanics at a garage in Haifa. One son was eighteen, the other twenty. When the war began, the Jews smuggled a bomb into their garage, and when it exploded—

But of course Isaac knew the story, and so do you. I asked him if the man cried.

"No," Isaac said. "But he was sad."

What could Isaac do for this man? He followed custom with a few comforting words and a request that God visit his vengeance upon the killers. After a while the father of the dead mechanics drifted off, and Isaac never saw him again.

At a few points in our conversations, I tried to draw Isaac out on the subject of his induction into the world of violence, the kind of questions reporters ask nowadays: How did it feel? Did he think about it afterward? He was polite, but I think he saw it as modern foolishness. Public introspection, the expression of regret in a few sentences of pathos—these were innovations of a later time. It wasn't the style of the Arab Section.

"We were given a job," he said of those days, "and I'm proud that I succeeded." That's all he would say. If I wanted to know what his success meant, I could stand up in his kitchen and look at the country out his seventh-floor window. People who'd been at the mercy of the majority in Warsaw, Berlin, Casablanca, and Aleppo had their own piece of land. Somewhere down in those streets were regular people going to the supermarket or riding the bus without knowing that they exist because once upon a time, on a Saturday morning in February 1948, two young men named Isaac and Yakuba ensured that a bomb disguised as an ambulance didn't blow up a movie theater.

Still, it seemed to me there was something about the story of the old man that made it different from Isaac's other stories. Perhaps the way it hinted at how fine the lines are between people—that this old man's sons, who were around Isaac's age and born in a city near his and spoke his language, could be Isaac, and Isaac's father could be the old refugee, or Isaac could be the old refugee himself. It's not the kind of thing he could have grasped when he heard the story at the kiosk, but the Isaac who recounted it to me was a father and a grandfather, much older than that old man with his story. When Isaac was finished, his hand moved in the air. It was just a small wave, but something I'd never seen him do before, as if to express our common helplessness in the face of fate, or to make something go away.

THE SECTION'S USUAL rendezvous point south of Beirut, the beach at Ouzai.

A black spot appeared in the distance offshore. It drew closer and assumed the shape of a dinghy. The soft splash of oars reached Isaac's ears. With him on the beach were Havakuk and the agent named Shimon, who'd been running the Damascus station.

Min hada? Isaac shouted across the water. Who's there? According to the agreed-upon exchange of passwords, the sailors were to answer, "Ibrahim," and then Isaac would ask in Arabic, "Is Mustafa with you?"

But when he shouted, *Min hada?* no one answered, and instead he heard excited Hebrew from the dinghy: Turn back! There were frantic splashes as the oarsmen tried to turn the boat around. No one had told them about any password. All they heard were words they didn't know in the enemy tongue.

Yob tvoyu mat, shouted Isaac, his favorite Russian curse, the one he used with Ashkenazim. And then in Hebrew: Come back!

Password or no password, he was going home tonight. The boat came back.

We thought you were a patrol, said the sailor in charge. We almost shot you.

The agents scrambled in, the sailors pulled at the oars, and the dinghy took them away from the lights of the Lebanese capital, away from the lives they'd lived for two years, toward the shape bobbing in the darkness offshore, the navy cutter *Palmach*. When the passengers were hauled on board, the ship set a course southward. On the left was the dark coastline, and on the right the open sea. It was the spring of 1950.

Yakuba had already been pulled out by this time, having pushed most energetically to leave. He even threatened to do it without permission: he'd simply drive down to the Lebanon-Israel border, he said, abandon the Oldsmobile, cross by himself, and catch a ride home. They knew he might really do it.

Gamliel was extracted separately. After he got back to Israel, he was assigned to officers' training in the new army. When he finished and reported back to the Arab Section, he was told it no longer existed. The fresh agents who'd been sent to Beirut, the ones who had trouble with Georgette, were recalled after a few months, and the unit was dismantled. Part of this was the general reform of the intelligence services in the young state, and internal arguments about which organization was in charge of what. But it may also have sunk in that while the Arab Section had created a new kind of agent, a One Who Becomes Like an Arab, and proved how useful that agent could be, more professionalism and sophistication were now needed. The Arab Section was the beginning, and the beginning was over.

After that, as Gamliel tells the story, he spent some time at loose ends, waiting for a new assignment, until one day he was at the army's sprawling camp in Tel Aviv when he ran into a woman he knew. She was serving as a clerk for two officers who had a little hut among the eucalyptus trees. The hut, she told him, was an outfit going by a generic name, the *reshut*, or "Authority." The name was later replaced with one equally generic: the "Institution," or *mossad*.

Gamliel signed up. He spent years as an Arab in Europe, first posing as an embassy clerk and later as a journalist. "Gamliel was

known in the intelligence community as one of Israel's most successful agents," a military historian said after his death in 2002.
"We never heard of him because he was never caught." He was
joined in the service by Yakuba the adventurer, Sam'an the teacher,
Rika the saboteur, and others you've met in these pages.

In the generation of our spies, Israeli intelligence was blessed
with thousands of Kims from Arab countries. But these people's
children spoke Hebrew, not Arabic. They were something new:
Israelis. The Israeli identity is increasingly Middle Eastern, but
the old languages and mannerisms are gone, as the Zionist movement always intended. Whatever the benefits this has brought the
Jewish people, it's been a curse for the spy services.

The strange word *mista'arvim*, Ones Who Become Like Arabs,
lives on in Hebrew, but with a slightly different meaning. Now it
denotes soldiers or police who carry out brief operations in Arab
guise, darting into Palestinian cities to arrest or kill suspects. They
don't live as Arabs, nor could they. "Being a One Who Becomes
Like an Arab," Sam'an wrote in the old days, "means appearing as
an Arab in every aspect: the way you look, talk, and behave, where
you live, and where you enjoy yourself, including the right cover,
papers, life story, and background." Today there's nearly no one in
Israel who can pull that off.

I'd like to know what Havakuk—the radioman, the watcher,
Ibrahim of the Haifa port—was thinking as he sailed home along
the coast that night in the spring of 1950. But of our four spies,
Havakuk left the least behind.

One of the first things he meant to do was to marry the fighter
Mira, who kept her promise to wait for him. The wedding was
held soon after Havakuk's return, and the whole Section came. At
around the same time, Havakuk was recruited by a new military

intelligence unit running Arab agents. One night the following year, 1951, he went to meet a contact on the desert border with Jordan, but it was a setup. The contact killed him and left him dead in the sand. Havakuk was twenty-four.

His young widow later married Yakuba. They had three children. The agent who once described himself as a "wild man" spent his life in and out of the secret services, changing identities and passports and, for one mission, his face, with plastic surgery. He was called to serve the country one last time in 2002, at seventy-eight years old, and when he died the following year he was eulogized as one of the great and colorful figures of Israel's intelligence world. I met Mira on her kibbutz, near a bougainvillea and a cotton field where the first tufts were just poking through. We drank coffee in a little red house that Yakuba built them with his own hands sixty-three years ago, at the beginning of the State of Israel, and of their life together.

EPILOGUE

'm watching a kiosk from a bench in Tel Aviv. I've been watching for an hour, though there's nothing mysterious about this kiosk. It's just a structure the size of a little room, with a striped awning and a lotto poster on one wall.

The kiosk is closed when I sit down on the bench a little after seven in the morning, but soon it opens with a few minutes of choreographed motion. An old woman with tidy hair shows up and unlocks a door. A middle-aged man in a black T-shirt brings out some chairs. A woman in a blue dress does something in the back. Chairs here. Table here. Ashtray on table. The three of them move around each other without speaking. They all know their part.

The man puts out a stand of potato chips. A metal shutter in one wall opens upward, revealing the top half of the old woman and the interior of the kiosk—a fridge with soft drinks, a counter with Bic lighters and lollipops. Elsewhere in the city are kiosks that sell cappuccino and gluten-free muffins to people who design websites, but not here. This is a simple kiosk by an elementary school. If this kiosk, with its people, were somehow lifted and dropped to the east of here, in Amman, or to the south in Alexandria, or to the west on one of the Greek islands, it would attract no attention. Business could continue without interruption.

A policeman ambles by and greets the old woman without stopping. A little girl with a big pink knapsack stands on her tiptoes and buys a pink pack of gum. A taxi driver takes L&Ms, his gruff familiarity with the kiosk lady suggesting that many packs of her L&Ms have crossed the counter in his direction over the years. The workday begins here on the eastern edge of the Mediterranean, an ordinary day at the end of the summer. The sea isn't visible behind the buildings but sends regards every so often with a weak draft of salty air. This is the time to be out in this part of the world, when the light is bright but not harsh, the heat still a few hours away. I ask the old lady for black coffee. She doesn't know me but calls me "sweetie" in Hebrew touched with Arabic, disappears into the back, and returns with a paper cup. I resume my surveillance.

I'm here because I'm trying to imagine that Beirut kiosk, kept from me by a hostile border and seven tumultuous decades. Like this one, it sits on a quiet street near a school. The sea, the same sea, is close enough to smell. On this morning that I'm picturing, in the late summer of 1948, clerks and laborers walk past the shuttered kiosk toward the clamor of horses, cars, and downtown trams. A few schoolchildren pass on their way to the Three Moons.

A click comes from inside. The window goes up.

Two young men look out from behind the counter. They move easily beside and around each other. They know each other very well. Both have mustaches. One wears glasses. I have a photograph of them grinning at the camera, hair slicked back and collars open. They seem capable of both humor and violence. If you ask their names, the bespectacled one says Abdul Karim, and the second says Ibrahim.

An Oldsmobile pulls up at the curb and another young man emerges. Like the first two, he's dark and has a mustache, but from the moment his legs hit the sidewalk you can tell he's cockier. His voice is louder. He's an adventurer. He strolls over to the pair at the counter and is greeted with handshakes and cheek kisses. This is Jamil. A fourth man walks by, Yussef. He seems more officious than the others, with an air of the intellectual. Don't be fooled by their relaxed manner. Five of their friends are in shallow graves, and fate isn't done with them yet. They're straining to understand what is happening around them and what will happen—through snippets of conversation, sentences in newspapers, clicking over a clothesline—but everything's veiled in fog. They shelter in the kiosk as if it were a lifeboat, the only solid object for miles. When I sit at this kiosk in the present I can almost see theirs. It would seem natural if one of them just walked by.

A SHORT DRIVE away from this kiosk is an ordinary apartment building. At the entrance are the names Katash, Rubinstein, Alexandrov, Kamakhji, and others brought by people who came here from somewhere else to become someone else. By one buzzer is the family name Isaac chose for himself when he took charge of his fate. An elevator barely larger than a telephone booth takes me to the seventh floor, and he's there at the door, a small man with a mustache and glasses, Isaac Shoshan, Zaki Shasho, Abdul Karim.

Isaac's career unfolded in several arms of Israeli intelligence. For a while he ran human smuggling routes for Jews fleeing Syria, one of which led from his hometown, Aleppo, through Beirut to a ship offshore, and then to the port at Haifa. He helped create a unit of commandos modeled on the British Special Air Service, meant to operate behind enemy lines. An Arabic song popular with the men in the unit's early days, the infectious call-and-response number "Musa Zein," was taught by Isaac while they all ran on the beach. He'd heard it as a child during Muslim wedding processions in the streets near his home in the Jewish Quarter.

Another old spy I know once watched Isaac debrief an agent at a safe house in Jerusalem. This was in the early years of the state. The second spy was a trainee at the time, and this was when he learned that intelligence men weren't what he'd seen in movies. Isaac wasn't threatening. He wasn't urbane. He was a man of gentle and meandering conversation, a psychologist without a high school diploma, a self-taught scholar of human nature and the Middle East.

Isaac's first wife, Yafa, fell ill and died young. Later he married Rachel, the little sister of some boys he knew from Aleppo. They've lived happily for many years in the same apartment building. He has a daughter in Tel Aviv and a son in New York and a grandson who plays the piano. On the ship bringing him home that night in the spring of 1950, he could have imagined none of it. He spent the trip not mulling the future or the past but vomiting over the rail.

At daybreak they steamed into Haifa. The sailors threw ropes, and the engine sputtered out. Isaac's companions parted from him, and he was on the dock by himself. There was no hero's welcome. There was no welcome at all, just a clerk's voucher for a night at an army hostel if he didn't have anywhere better to sleep. He didn't. He thought someone from the Palmach might be there to hear stories, but there was no Palmach anymore. He was in the same city he'd left two years before on the bus with the refugees—and in a different city, with new people in the old homes. It was the same country he'd left in the chaos of the war, and a different one, where he'd never been. He was the same person and a different person.

In one of our final conversations for this book, when Isaac was ninety-three, he told me that he found himself thinking about his mother. He sounded surprised, as if this hadn't happened before. Her name was Mazal. She died in childbirth when he was seven, in old Aleppo, in that other world that existed before the twentieth century picked everything up and scattered it.

He doesn't know what she looked like, and this troubles him. Sometimes her image seems within reach and then slips away. There are no photographs. If he concentrates he can see her outline, as if he's looking up at her and she's lit from behind. Maybe the light is Aleppo sunshine. Maybe she's about to lift him into her arms.

His mother is thin and tall. She wears a little gold pendant. But he can't see her face or hear her voice. Isaac wonders whether she called him by the same name as everyone else, or whether she had a special name for him, one that only she used. What did his mother call him? He needs to know, but he can't remember.

NOTES ON SOURCES

The epigraph is from an essay by William Boyd titled "Why John le Carré Is More Than a Spy Novelist," in the *New Statesman* (October 21, 2015).

Preface

My first interview with Isaac Shoshan was in February 2011 at his home in Bat-Yam. My last was in July 2016. We were introduced by the retired intelligence officer Rafi Sutton, who played a central role in *The Aleppo Codex* (Algonquin Books, 2012). I published a short version of Isaac's story in an article titled "Our Man in Beirut" in the *Times of Israel* (April 15, 2013).

The observation that about half the Jewish population of Israel has roots in the Islamic world—with the caveat that intermarriage among Jewish Israelis is blurring the statistics—is from an interview with the Israeli demographer Sergio DellaPergola of Hebrew University in May 2012.

Chapter 1: The Scout

The details of the departure of Gamliel Cohen ("Yussef") from Haifa on January 17, 1948, are drawn from a 205-page transcript of Gamliel's oral recollections recorded by Beit Yigal Allon and made available to me by the Palmach archive, Beit Ha-Palmach, Tel Aviv. The transcript is undated but appears to be from the late 1990s. Additional details are from Gamliel's published history of the Arab Section, *Ha-Mistaarvim Ha-Rishonim* [Under cover: The untold story of the Palmach's under cover Arab unit] (Tel Aviv: Defense Ministry Press and Galili Institute for Defense Studies, 2002).

For help in re-creating the landscape of Haifa in 1948, I'm grateful to Yigal Greiver of the Haifa Historical Society and to Jafar Farah of the Mossawa Center in Haifa.

"To the noble Arab public: Beware the fifth column!" The poster, dated December 12, 1947, is described in Muhammad Nimr el-Khatib, *Min Athar el-Nakba* [From the fragments of the catastrophe] (Damascus: Al-Matba'ah al-Umumiyah, 1951). Parts of the Arabic book, including the text of posters put up by the Arab leadership in Haifa, were translated into Hebrew after the war in a volume published by the Israeli army, *Be-Einey Oyev: Shlosha Pirsumim Araviim al Milhemet Hakomemiyut* [Through enemy eyes: Three Arab descriptions of the Independence War], translated by Captain S. Sabag (Tel Aviv: Ma'arachot Publishing, 1954). Additional sections of el-Khatib's book were translated for me from the Arabic by Yehonatan Gorenberg.

"Noble Arabs! The national committee is sparing no effort": That poster, also described in el-Khatib, *Min Athar el-Nakba*, is dated December 8, 1947.

The photograph of Gamliel, taken in Beirut in 1950, appears courtesy of the Palmach photo archive.

"The shouts of the waiters and curses of the card-players": From an intelligence report written by Havakuk Cohen ("Ibrahim") of the Arab Section, spring/summer 1947. From the Palmach files in the archives of the kibbutz movement at Yad Tabenkin.

The intelligence briefs on various cafés are from "Batei ha-cafeh ha-arviim be-Haifa beshalhei tkufat ha-mandat al pi sikrei ha-esek shel sherut ha-yediot shel ha-Hagana" [Arab cafés in Haifa in the twilight of the Mandate period according to Hagana intelligence's survey of businesses], by Yair Safran and Tamir Goren, in *Haifa: The Newsletter of the Haifa Historical Society* 12 (December 2014). The intelligence survey is undated.

A photograph of the transcript of the conversation among Arab militiamen in Jaffa regarding the fate of the two captured spies appears in the book *Vesodam Lakchu Elei Kever* [They took their secret to the grave], a memorial volume self-published in 2015 by the families of David Shamash and Gideon Ben-David, kept in the Palmach archive. The transcript of the tapped conversation (December 20, 1947) was discovered by Professor Yoav Gelber of the University of Haifa in the Ben-Gurion Archives; bureaucratic confusion seems to be the reason it ended up there, rather than with the other Arab Section documents in the archives of the Palmach, Hagana, IDF, or kibbutz movement.

Details on the disappearance of the "peddler," the nineteen-year-old Arab Section agent Nissim Attiyeh, are from an interview with two officers from the IDF unit Eitan, which searches for missing soldiers, on January 31, 2017. Attiyeh's body was never found and the file remains open. The sources differ on whether he was disguised as a peddler or a barber on the day he vanished; the IDF file says the latter, and Gamliel's version says the former.

The report from the Arabic newspaper *Al-Shaab* (December 24, 1947) is cited in Zvika Dror, *Ha-Mistaarvim Shel Ha-Palmach* [The "Arabists" of the Palmach] (Tel Aviv: Defense Ministry Press, 1986). I've referred to Dror's book as the "official history." The Arab Section agent in question—the fourth captured that week and the only one to survive—was Shmuel (Sami) Mamroud. He gave his own account of his capture at a reunion of Arab Section veterans in January

1985. A transcript of the meeting can be found in the Palmach archive, as well
as in the Yad Tabenkin archive (with handwritten annotations by Gamliel
Cohen).

The fighter Sabari, who died with thirty-four others when their unit was
ambushed on January 16, 1948, was David Sabari, seventeen, from Jerusalem.

Chapter 2: At Camp

The photograph shows the Arab Section camp at Kibbutz Yagur circa 1946;
by the time Gamliel returned from Beirut, the camp had moved to a different
kibbutz, Givat Hashlosha. Courtesy of the Palmach photo archive.

The description of the men at camp is from my interviews with Isaac; from
Gamliel's oral testimony and published account; and from the transcript of
a long interview with Yakuba Cohen ("Jamil"), conducted on behalf of Beit
Yigal Allon by Iza Dafni in March and April 2001. The full Hebrew name of the
teacher Sam'an was Shimon Somech. Dahud's name was David Mizrahi. Ezra
was Ezra Afgin, who changed his family name to the Hebrew "Horin." Rika is
Eliyahu Rika. Bokai is Yaakov Bokai.

"An old gramophone": From Eliyahu Rika, *Parpar Ha-shachar* [Butterfly of the
Dawn] (Tel Aviv: Yorikel Press, 1987).

The photograph of the backgammon players appears courtesy of the Palmach
photo archive.

"Independence is not given but taken by force": Arab Section report (November
1946) by Gamliel and Isaac, who attended an Arab nationalist rally in Nablus.
The speaker was Faik Inbatawi. From Gamliel's published account.

"The sermon didn't include a single sentence about politics": Arab Section
report from the village of Yahudiya, June 30, 1947, in the Hagana archive.

"This movie has left a deep impression in their hearts": Havakuk's report from
Haifa, spring/summer 1947, in the kibbutz movement archive at Yad Tabenkin.

"I saw a group of twenty or thirty kids": Arab Section report from Haifa, June
16, 1947, in the Hagana archive.

Isaac's Arabic proverbs were collected in *Pitgam Yashan-Shoshan* [Shoshan's old
proverbs], compiled by his daughter Etti Yodan, self-published in Tel Aviv, 2016.

"Private car no. 6544": Arab Section report from Jaffa, December 1, 1947, in the
Hagana archive.

Chapter 3: The Garage

The description of the mission at the Abu Sham garage in Haifa in February
1948 is drawn from my interviews with Isaac and from Yakuba's oral testimony.

Additional details are from Dror's official history and from Gamliel's published account.

Details on Yakuba's early life are from his oral testimony.

The photograph of Yakuba (date and location unclear) appears courtesy of the Palmach photo archive.

A Minox that belonged to a civilian they knew: From Dror's official history. The camera's owner was Aaron Tziling, a member of Kibbutz Ein Harod, later minister of agriculture. According to Dror's account the agents were told in jest, "We don't care if you come back or not, as long as the camera does."

"Contact with the Arabs has been severely damaged": The official is Yaakov Shimoni, quoted in Ian Black and Benny Morris, *Israel's Secret Wars: A History of Israel's Intelligence Services* (New York: Grove Press, 1991).

"We must assume that they can also disguise themselves as Jews": From a document (undated) in the Hagana archive, titled "Report on Arab Gangs in Central and Southern Palestine."

When the Nazis dropped a sabotage team of Arabs and Germans into Palestine in 1944: A description of this incident can be found in Michael Bar-Zohar and Eitan Haber, *The Quest for the Red Prince* (London: Weidenfeld and Nicolson, 1983).

"Any stranger, even an Arab, who appeared in Jaffa": From a brief summary of the Section's history written by Sam'an (Shimon Somech) for internal use, dated June 17, 1971. From the Hagana archive.

The number of fatalities in the Abu Sham blast is unclear. According to a Palmach document cited by Black and Morris in *Israel's Secret Wars*, the number was thirty; according to Gamliel's published account, the number was twenty; according to the official Hagana history, the number was five. According to a poster put up by the Hagana immediately after the attack, "The garage was destroyed and its surroundings damaged, several Arabs were killed and dozens wounded." A search in the extensive Arabic newspaper archives at Tel Aviv University's Moshe Dayan Center for Middle Eastern and African Studies failed to turn up an account of the incident or casualty figures from the Arab side.

Chapter 4: The Watcher (1)

The arrival of the illegal refugee ship *Hannah Senesh* on Christmas Day, 1945, is recounted by both Gamliel and Yakuba in their oral testimonies.

Nathan Alterman's poem "Ne'um tshuva le-rav-hovlim italki aharei leil horada" [A speech in reply to an Italian captain after a night of disembarkation] was written after the arrival of the *Hannah Senesh* and first published in the newspaper *Davar* on January 15, 1946.

"People who have seen death and fear nothing": Arab Section report from Jaffa, June 16, 1947, from the Hagana archive.

The details of the daily life of "Ibrahim" in Haifa are from Havakuk's report from the city, spring/summer 1947, in the kibbutz movement archives at Yad Tabenkin.

Chapter 5: Tiger

Sources on Arab Haifa in 1948 include Benny Morris, *1948: A History of the First Arab-Israeli War* (New Haven, CT: Yale University Press, 2008); Tamir Goren, *Haifa ha-aravit be-tashach* [The fall of Arab Haifa in 1948] (Tel Aviv: Ben-Gurion University of the Negev with Defense Ministry Press, 2006); Information Service intelligence reports in the Hagana archive; and el-Khatib, *Min Athar el-Nakba*.

The agent who described praying with seven hundred worshippers in Jaffa was Shem-Tov Aloni, who spoke at the Arab Section reunion in 1985 (transcript in the Palmach archive).

Gamliel's description of Nimr el-Khatib as a "fire-and-brimstone inciter," and his musings about committing violence in the mosque, are from his oral testimony.

Gamliel's report from the Muslim Brotherhood rally (July 10, 1947) is in the Hagana archive. The identity of the report's author isn't clear from the document, but in his oral testimony Gamliel says it was him.

"If we control Tel Aviv and the cities of the coastal plain": Azriel Carlebach writing in the Hebrew newspaper *Maariv*, April 22, 1948.

The Palmach document describing the attempted assassination is from the Palmach files at the kibbutz movement archives, Yad Tabenkin. The document (undated but presumably from late February or early March 1948) is titled "Report on the execution of Operation Starling against Sheikh Nimr el-Khatib." Operation Starling (Hebrew: *mivtza zarzir*) was a broader plan to assassinate leaders of the Arab war effort.

Chapter 6: Isaac

The account of Isaac's childhood is from his interviews with me.

"Are held in still greater contempt than the Christians": From Alexander Russell, *The Natural History of Aleppo*, published in London in 1756, cited in Norman Stillman, *The Jews of Arab Lands: A History and Source Book* (Philadelphia: Jewish Publication Society, 1979).

The photograph of Isaac and his siblings appears courtesy of Isaac Shoshan.

"The masts on the rooftops then": Leah Goldberg's poem "Hamasa Hakatzar Beyoter" [The shortest journey], describing Tel Aviv in 1935, appeared in her collection *Im Ha-Laila Ha-zeh* [With this night] (Merhavia: Sifriat Ha-Po'alim, 1964). Translation mine. Appears with permission of Hakibbutz Hameuchad-Sifriat Poalim Publishing, Bnei Brak, Israel.

"Home is a name, a word": From Dickens's *The Life and Adventures of Martin Chuzzlewit* (London: Chapman & Hall, 1844).

Benny Marshak's fable about the cliff appears in Dror's official history.

"Their self-confidence, nurtured by a mixture of ignorance": From Anita Shapira, *Yigal Allon, Native Son: A Biography*, translated by Evelyn Abel (Philadelphia: University of Pennsylvania Press, 2008).

"Throw yourself on the scales": Yitzhak Sadeh's words are cited in Haim Gouri and Haim Hefer, *Mishpachat Ha-Palmach* [The Palmach family], 4th ed. (Tel Aviv: Yediot Books, 1977).

The account of the meeting at the kibbutz with Marshak and Sam'an is from Isaac's interviews with me, with additional detail from Dror's history.

The description of Arab Section training is drawn mainly from Isaac's interviews with me, with additional detail from Gamliel's oral testimony and published account, and from Yakuba's oral testimony.

Both photographs of Sam'an (Shimon Somech) appear courtesy of the Palmach photo archive.

"This was Sam'an": From Yakuba's oral testimony.

Sam'an's role in the Eli Cohen operation is detailed in Shmuel Segev, *Boded Be-Damesek* [Alone in Damascus: The life and death of Eli Cohen], rev. ed. (Jerusalem: Keter Books, 2012).

The skepticism among Jewish intelligence officers about the efficacy of the Arab Section concept is mentioned in Dror's official history.

"Brought back useful information about Arab morale": From Black and Morris, *Israel's Secret Wars*.

"We didn't learn it from anyone": Arab Section veteran Yair Harari ("Subhi"), speaking at the veterans' reunion in 1985 (transcript in the Palmach archive).

"Must first be the son of an eastern Jewish community": This quote from Sam'an appears in Gamliel's published account.

Nine of every ten Jews in Palestine came from Europe: Morris, *1948*.

The poverty of the Palmach, and the occasional inability to pay for food or accommodations, are described by Gamliel in his oral testimony.

The number of members in the Section fluctuated, and many dozens passed through over the years. At the 1985 reunion the number of invitees was forty-nine, a figure that obviously doesn't include members who died in 1948 or subsequently. But the number of active agents at any given time was much smaller; the files show that at the outbreak of the Independence War in late 1947, their number was no more than a dozen.

"The *sabras* are notorious for their complete disregard of form": S. D. Goitein, *Jews and Arabs: Their Contacts through the Ages* (New York: Schocken Books, 1955).

"Isn't just a young man with dark skin": From an internal document by Sam'an, cited in Yaakov Markovitzki, *Ha-yehidot ha-yabashtiot ha-meyuchadot shel ha-Palmach* [Palmach special ground units] (Tel Aviv: Defense Ministry Press, 1989).

"The bespectacled Isaac Shoshan, a rope in his hand": From Gamliel's published account.

The photograph of Mira appears courtesy of Mira Cohen. I interviewed Mira at Kibbutz Alonim in August 2016.

The songs from the Arab Section campfires, and the Arabic words that entered Hebrew through Palmach slang, appear in Gouri and Hefer, *Mishpachat Ha-Palmach*. The lyrics of "From Beyond the River" ("Me-Ever La-Nahar," words by Shaul Tchernichovsky, melody by Anton Rubinstein) appear in the same volume. The translation of the song here is mine. The version by the army troupe (Nachal Entertainment Troupe, 1972) can be found on YouTube.

"I felt the insult after a campfire that ended at dawn": From Yehuda Nini's 1971 essay "Hirhurim al ha-hurban ha-shlishi" [Ruminations on the third destruction], in the kibbutz movement journal *Shdemot* 41.

"They'd come, and we'd dress like Arabs": From Gamliel's oral testimony.

"Sometimes I thought that more than our bonfire gave off sparks": From a memoir by the early Arab Section veteran Moshe Adaki, *Be-esh netzura* [With guarded fire] (Tel Aviv: Am Oved, 1975).

Chapter 7: Operation Starling

Details of the attempted assassination from Isaac's perspective are drawn mainly from my interviews with Isaac, with additional details from a book he cowrote with Rafi Sutton about their years in the service of Israeli intelligence, *Anshei ha-sod veha-seter* [Men of secrets, men of mystery] (Tel Aviv: Edanim, 1990). Additional details are from the Palmach document describing Operation Starling, from the Yad Tabenkin archive.

The date of Muhammad Nimr el-Khatib's departure for Syria was February 15, 1948, according to his account in *Min Athar el-Nakba*. The attack took place upon his return four days later, on February 19.

All quotes from Muhammad Nimr el-Khatib's account of the attack are in *Min Athar el-Nakba*, translated for me from the Arabic by Yehonatan Gorenberg. I obtained the only copy of the memoir that I could find in a public collection anywhere in the world—at the library of the Palestinian university An-Najah in the West Bank city of Nablus—with the help of two Palestinian journalists, who brought the book to Jaffa for a few hours to allow me to photograph it.

ISAAC: "We set out early in the morning to the ambush spot" and "Just as doubt crept into my heart": From Isaac's book with Rafi Sutton.

PALMACH REPORT: "At 10 o'clock the car passed": From the Operation Starling document at the Yad Tabenkin archive.

ISAAC: "I gave them the signal—a handkerchief": From my interview with Isaac.

ISAAC: "We passed, slowed down, and forced the sheikh's car": From Isaac's book with Rafi Sutton.

MALINKI: "We fired bursts at the vehicle": From Tzadok Eshel, *Ma'archot ha-Hagana be-Haifa* [Hagana battles in Haifa] (Tel Aviv: Defense Ministry Press, 1978). The name Malinki, "little" in Russian, is a nickname; the gunman's identity is unrecorded.

ISAAC: "I wanted to get out with the pistol": From my interview with Isaac.

The report from *El-Difaa* (February 20, 1948) appears in el-Khatib, *Min Athar el-Nakba*.

Chapter 8: Cedar

The description of Gamliel's time in Beirut, of his childhood in Damascus, and of his first months in Palestine are from his oral testimony.

Agents running clandestine immigration from Iraq used the code name *artzi* to mean the Land of Israel: From Shlomo Hillel, *Operation Babylon: Jewish Clandestine Activity in the Middle East 1946-51* (Glasgow: William Collins, 1988).

One member of the Hagana command, a Frenchman, had the code name Frenchman: from Black and Morris, *Israel's Secret Wars*.

Gamliel's report on the Muslim Brotherhood rally in Haifa (July 10, 1947) is from the Hagana archive, as is his report on a meeting of Arab Communists in the city (May 13, 1947) and his report from a nationalist rally at Sheikh Mounis (June 26, 1947).

"Because I was the one who wanted to join them": From Gamliel's oral testimony.

Details of Gamliel's later life are from a short movie about him screened at a conference at the Palmach Museum on February 21, 2012, a decade after his death; a video of the conference is in the Palmach archive. Additional details from an interview in April 2018, with his wife, Aliza Cohen, and his daughter Mira Shamir (born "Samira el-Hamed" while her father was undercover in Europe). Batsheva's inscription is from Gamliel's oral testimony.

"The balance of the fighting seems to have turned much in favor of the Arabs": British High Commissioner Alan Cunningham in a report to the colonial secretary on April 3, 1948, cited in Morris, *1948*.

Poza was Haim Poznanski, killed at twenty-one in the battle of Nebi Samwil (April 23, 1948).

Descriptions of the death of Abd el-Qader el-Husseini at Qastel can be found, with some minor variations, in numerous sources. I've relied on the most recent account, Danny Rubinstein, *Ze anachnu oh hem* [The battle on the Kastel: Twenty-four hours that changed the course of the 1948 war between Palestinians and Israelis) (Tel Aviv: Aliyat Ha-Gag Books, 2017).

"Similarly Leamas, without relinquishing the power of invention": John le Carré, *The Spy Who Came In from the Cold* (London: Victor Gollancz, 1963).

Chapter 9: The Watcher (2)

This chapter is drawn from the report filed by Havakuk ("Ibrahim") immediately after the fall of Haifa on April 22, 1948. The entire report was read aloud by Gamliel at a meeting of Arab Section veterans at Kibbutz Givat Hashlosha on April 10, 1969, and thus fortuitously survives in the transcript of that meeting in the Palmach archive; I could find no trace of the original.

"To the fighting nation": The text of this poster, dated March 20, 1948, appears in el-Khatib, *Min Athar el-Nakba*.

"Refugees fleeing the path of the advancing columns": From Walid Khalidi, "The Fall of Haifa Revisited," originally published in *Middle East Forum* 10 (1959), reprinted in *Journal of Palestine Studies* 37, no. 3 (Spring 2008).

"Stay in your place. Reinforce your position": The text of this poster, dated December 12, 1947, appears in el-Khatib, *Min Athar el-Nakba*.

"The Arab hospitals are full of dead and wounded": Report from the Carmeli Brigade, April 22, 1948, in Benny Morris, *The Birth of the Palestinian Refugee Problem Revisited* (Cambridge: Cambridge University Press, 2004).

Haifa's Jewish mayor was at the port begging people to stay: Morris, *The Birth of the Palestinian Refugee Problem Revisited*, and in other sources.

"The sky was on fire crackling with shots, bombs and explosions": From Ghassan Kanafani's novella *Returning to Haifa*, in *Palestine's Children:*

Returning to Haifa and Other Stories, translated by Barbara Harlow and Karen E. Riley (Boulder, CO: Lynne Rienner, 2000).

Chapter 10: Kim

"From Philhellenic dons to well-connected thugs": From Antony Beevor, *Crete: The Battle and the Resistance* (London: John Murray, 1991).

I saw the British maps for the planned last stand at Haifa in the Second World War during a visit to the Haifa Historical Society in 2016.

Yonatan Ben-Nahum's essay on the origins of the idea of "Ones Who Become Like Arabs," the most insightful piece of writing I found on the subject, seems never to have been published; I happened upon a typed draft in a file at the kibbutz movement archives at Yad Tabenkin. Ben-Nahum, a highly regarded Israeli author born in 1941, published his second and last book in 1999 before being disabled by a stroke that rendered him unable to communicate. I spoke to his brother, the historian Yizhar Ben-Nahum, in April 2018, but was unable to ascertain the origins of the essay.

Nicholas Hammond, an explosives expert recruited by the SOE from Cambridge, later a respected scholar of ancient Greece, recounted his wartime experience in *Venture Into Greece: With the Guerrillas, 1943–44* (London: William Kimber, 1983). Members of the early Arab Section remembered Hammond with admiration as someone who provided crucial training and backing for the unit at its inception. Hammond, however, makes no mention of the Section at all in his memoir, which focuses on Greece and makes only passing mention of his time in Palestine.

Patrick Leigh Fermor, famous as a travel writer, recounted his time with the Cretan resistance in *Abducting a General: The Kreipe Operation and SOE in Crete* (London: John Murray, 2014).

"In the evenings we sat around the campfire and sang German songs": Yehuda Brieger, quoted in *Magen Ba-seter* [Secret shield], edited by Zerubavel Gilad with Galia Yardeni (Jerusalem: Jewish Agency Press, 1948).

Chapter 11: Exceptional Opportunities

The memo from "Hillel," Yisrael Galili, is from the Arab Section files at the IDF archive at Tel Ha-Shomer, dated May 6, 1948. Oddly, the numeral "6" is handwritten, while the rest of the note is typed. This peculiarity is worth pointing out because Dror's history cites an entry in David Ben-Gurion's diary from the same day, May 6, according to which two agents had left two days earlier. Assuming Ben-Gurion was referring to Isaac and Havakuk, that would put the date of their departure on May 4, or thirteen days after the fall of Haifa on April 22. In that case, it would seem that the "6" on Hillel's memo is an error, and that it was written before May 4.

"Carcass city": The observer was David Ben-Gurion, who visited on May 1. Cited in Shai Fogelman, "Port in a Storm," *Haaretz* weekend magazine, June 3, 2011.

The account of Isaac and Havakuk's departure is from my interviews with Isaac.

"I will stand on my watch": Book of Havakuk 2:1–3, from the Jewish Publication Society translation (Philadelphia: JPS, 1999).

"A terrible mood would attack me": Havakuk in his report from Haifa in the spring/summer of 1947, in the Yad Tabenkin archive.

Sam'an stressed his desire for the long-term "planting" of agents, and his disappointment that this wasn't done more before the 1948 war, in a five-page internal document on the Arab Section from June 1956, in the Yad Tabenkin archive.

Yakuba recounted his own time undercover in Haifa in his oral testimony.

The ad for Teltsch House (Haifa's "most beautiful and well-appointed hotel") ran in the Hebrew newspaper *Davar* on July 12, 1937. From the online archive Historical Jewish Press, National Library, Jerusalem.

Fawzi al-Qawuqji's promise to wage "total war" against the Jews and to "murder, wreck, and ruin everything in our way" is cited in Morris, *1948*.

Chapter 12: The Fall of Israel

The description of what Isaac saw when crossing out of Palestine and into Lebanon is from my interviews with him.

"You couldn't do anything but believe in these people": From my interview with Mira Cohen at Kibbutz Alonim, August 2016. Mira's brother, Ben-Zion Mizrahi, was killed at the battle of Nebi Samwil on April 23, 1948. He was twenty-seven.

"It is impossible in the enchantment of its setting": From Jan Morris, *A Writer's World* (London: Faber & Faber, 2004).

In describing Beirut at the time, including the landscape of the city center and the city's nightclubs, I've made use of Samir Kassir, *Beirut*, translated by M. B. DeBevoise (Berkeley: University of California Press, 2010).

"Sought to re-create the ceremonies of the Parisian night": From Kassir, *Beirut*.

There were rumors that you could tell a spy by a mark on his back or inside his mouth: From Gamliel's oral testimony.

Such people had been uncovered in the Houran region of Syria and elsewhere: From a fourteen-page report handwritten by Gamliel in the Arab Section files at the IDF archive. The report, undated, is in a file from the summer of 1949, but the content suggests it was written earlier, perhaps in the fall of 1948.

The photograph of David Mizrahi and Ezra Afgin (Horin) in Egyptian captivity appears courtesy of the Palmach archive.

Ezra's grin was gone and he had blue marks under his eyes: From Gamliel's published account.

An Egyptian communiqué said they were caught near an army camp with a jar containing typhus and dysentery bacteria: From a Reuters report (picked up by *Yediot Ahronot* on May 25, 1948, in the online archive of *Yediot Ahronot* at the National Library in Jerusalem) citing an official statement from the Egyptian army. According to Israeli military records, the two spies were executed in Gaza three months later, on August 22.

The incident at the Bedouin camp in Galilee happened around July 1947. This description is from my interviews with Isaac; from a written version recorded by his daughter, Etti Yodan, in October 2006; and from an account from Isaac at the reunion of Arab Section veterans in 1985 (transcript in the Palmach archive).

"The Arab Legion conquers Jerusalem" and "First military report broadcast in Lebanon": Headlines in the newspaper *Al-Hayat* on May 16, 1948. Editions of the newspaper (and of all Arabic newspapers mentioned in this chapter) are preserved in the Arab press archive of the Dayan Center, translated for me by Yehonatan Gorenberg.

The caricature in *Beirut al-Masaa* appeared on May 31, 1948.

A ceremony lasting thirty-two minutes: Morris, *1948*. The three settlements that fell the same morning were Revadim, Ein Tzurim, and Masu'ot Yitzhak, all of them in the Etzion Bloc south of Jerusalem.

"To be out of wireless communication": Xan Fielding quoted in Beevor, *Crete*.

"Arab artillery follows the evacuation of Jewish neighborhoods" and "The last obstacle": Headlines from *Al-Hayat*, May 23, 1948.

"We looked at each other, Havakuk and I": From Isaac's book with Rafi Sutton.

Chapter 13: The Three Moons Kiosk

"During the session all roads leading to parliament": From an Arab Section radio transmission (January 27, 1949), in the log of messages preserved in the Arab Section files at the IDF archives.

Details on the treatment of the refugees by the Lebanese and the UN, and on the mood in Lebanon in those months, are from Gamliel's fourteen-page report in the IDF archive.

Details on the daily routine at the kiosk are from my interviews with Isaac.

"The inside of the store is strategic for us": From an undated radio message from Isaac to headquarters, cited in Gamliel's published account.

Beirut is undefended against air attack: From a summary of intelligence reports from Beirut and Damascus, August 4, 1948, in the IDF archive.

The Syrian army's order for one thousand binoculars, the arrival of the US merchantman in Beirut, and the Italian weapons shipment: From an intelligence report in the IDF archive, February 22, 1949.

The list of goods reaching Beirut ("100 tons of leather," etc.): From an intelligence report in the IDF archive, dated February 6, 1949, credited to the intelligence office Shin Mem 10.

Report on the Rayak airfield: From an intelligence report in the IDF archive dated September 8, 1949, source "an informer."

The coordinates of various targets in Beirut are from an appendix to Gamliel's fourteen-page report in the IDF archive.

"Because of the possibility that the enemy can listen in": Message from Arab Section headquarters to Beirut, December 10, 1948, 6:15 a.m., in the IDF archive.

"The enemy has a listening station": Message from Arab Section headquarters to Beirut, December 16, 1948, 6:00 a.m., in the IDF archive.

Headquarters recommended that Havakuk buy an appliance: Message from Arab Section headquarters to Beirut, August 13, 1949, in the IDF archive.

Chapter 14: Casino Méditerranée

Details of Yakuba's departure for Beirut, of his childhood, and of his early years in the Palmach are from his oral testimony.

The incident in which Yakuba took part around 1943—the castration of a suspected rapist in the town of Beisan—was well known at the time and is mentioned in numerous sources, though key details have become muddled, notably the name of the suspect and the date. The most thorough account I found was an article by the journalist Amos Nevo in *Yediot Ahronot* (April 30, 1993); according to the article, the incident probably took place in June 1943, and the name of the target was Muhammad Tawash.

The photograph (undated) of Yakuba in the uniform of the Najada militia and the photograph of Yakuba with the Oldsmobile appear courtesy of the Palmach photo archive. The photograph of Isaac and Havakuk in the Oldsmobile appears courtesy of Isaac Shoshan.

Chapter 15: Hitler's Yacht

Background on Hitler's yacht *Aviso Grille* is from a profile of the ship by Revel Barker, former Fleet Street reporter and managing editor at Mirror Group Newspapers. Barker, with whom I corresponded in April 2018, researched the history of the *Grille* after purchasing one of the yacht's small boats, *Grillet*, printing his findings in 2001 in *The Story of Motorboot 1*, a self-published volume intended for visitors to the boat (available online at http://strangevehicles.greyfalcon.us/AVISO%20GRILLE.htm).

"The action against the 'Grille' is set by the army's general staff": Message from Arab Section headquarters to Beirut, November 17, 1948, 6:00 a.m., in the IDF archive.

The photograph of the *Grille* at harbor appears courtesy of the Palmach photo archive.

"Confirm that you understand everything": Message from Arab Section headquarters to Beirut, November 19, 1948, 6:00 a.m., in the IDF archive.

A sighting of German Tiger tanks in the service of the Egyptian army: According to the intelligence report in the IDF archive (September 24, 1948), four were spotted by an informer on July 19, 1948, and three by a different source on August 25.

The arrival of twenty-five Wehrmacht officers, "experts on artillery, tanks and air warfare," and the possible appearance of twenty-five hundred former German soldiers: From a report in the IDF archive (January 20, 1949), credited to "a serious source" but passed on "with all due reservations."

"Working on the *Grille*, the Führer's private yacht": From Gamliel's published account; according to his source notes, the letter is in "the author's archive."

The yacht . . . now belonged to a Lebanese businessman . . . the ship was bound for the service of King Farouk: From the Israeli navy's official account of the operation in Lieutenant Commander Eliezer Tal, *Mivtza'ei cheil ha-yam be-milhemet ha-komemiyut* [Naval operations in the Israel War of Independence] (Tel Aviv: Israel Defense Forces, Ma'arachot Press, 1964). The Lebanese businessman was George Arida.

"Significantly increase the forces of the Egyptian navy": From the navy's official account by Eliezer Tal.

"It was as if the tormentor, in his grave": Rika, *Parpar Ha-shachar*.

"The sweet taste of revenge": From Gamliel's published account.

"Due to moon and sea conditions": Message from Arab Section headquarters to Beirut, November 22, 1948, 6:00 a.m., in the IDF archive.

The Jews had become the targets of "wild behavior": From Gamliel's fourteen-page report to headquarters, in the IDF archive.

"Once an envoy of ours in an Arab country": This quote from Yigal Allon, unearthed by Zvika Dror, appeared in an article by Meir Hareuveni in *Maariv*, March 16, 1987.

"You understand of course that we cannot change our operational principles": Message from Arab Section headquarters to Beirut, January 1, 1949, 7:00 a.m., in the IDF archive.

Gamliel's account of seeing his brothers and parents is from his published account.

Isaac's account of his return to Aleppo in the early summer of 1948 is from his interviews with me.

Another man I know from Aleppo remembered the rumor: This is Rafi Sutton, then a child in Aleppo, later an Israeli intelligence operative.

Gamliel's memory of passing a synagogue and hearing the prayers is from the short biographical film about him screened at the 2012 conference at the Palmach Museum, a video of which is available at the Palmach archive. Additional detail is from my interview with his widow, Aliza Cohen, in April 2018.

Yakuba's account of meeting a Jewish merchant from Damascus in early 1948 is from his oral testimony.

Chapter 16: The Saboteur

"The password on the beach when the boat arrives": Message from Arab Section headquarters to Beirut, November 24, 6:00 a.m., in the IDF archive.

"The mission will be carried out today": Message from Arab Section headquarters to Beirut, November 29, 6:15 a.m., in the IDF archive.

Details of the mission from Eliyahu Rika's perspective are from his memoir *Parpar Ha-shachar* and from a report he filed immediately after the operation, quoted extensively in the official navy account by Eliezer Tal. Rika, still an intelligence operative when Tal's account was published in 1964, is identified only as the "explosives expert." Additional details from an interview with Rika, age 89, in Tel Aviv in 2019.

"The ampoule slipped the whole time…": From Rika's report, cited in the navy account by Tal.

"Congratulations are sent to you": Message from Arab Section headquarters to Beirut, December 1, 6:15 a.m., in the IDF archive.

"Caused a flame 30 meters high": From a newspaper report in *Al-Hayat* cited in the official navy account by Tal. The date of the explosion, according to Tal, was December 17, 1948, or eighteen days after the operation.

The strange fate of the *Grille*'s toilet was recounted by Alexander Aciman in *Tablet* ("Hitler's Toilet Is in New Jersey," January 29, 2013). According to Aciman, when the yacht was broken up for scrap by New Jersey shipyard owner Harry Doan in the early 1950s, pieces of the ship—including teak paneling, a table, a window, and the toilet—were salvaged by residents in Florence and nearby towns. The toilet was in an auto repair shop owned by Greg Kohlfeldt until 2015, when Kohlfeldt sold it (for "under $5,000") to an unidentified British man (Gabriela Geselowitz, "Hitler's Toilet Sold," *Tablet*, April 20, 2015). According to an article in the *Mirror* (Warren Manger, "The Man Who Salvaged Hitler's Toilet," May 8, 2017), the current owner is Bruce Crompton, a British TV personality and collector.

Chapter 17: The Gallows

"If you attach a cone to the wall of a room": Message from Arab Section headquarters to Beirut, December 4, 1948, in the IDF archive.

Details of Yakuba's plan for the Tripoli refinery are from his oral testimony and from my interviews with Isaac.

Gamliel's consultations with a coffee reader and fortune teller are recounted in his oral testimony. His experiences as a member of the SSNP are recounted in his oral testimony and published account.

The photograph of the SSNP rally (March 1, 1949), taken by Gamliel, appears courtesy of the Palmach archive.

"Thought his job was to get up in the morning and read the paper" and "I was a wild man": From Yakuba's oral testimony.

The description of the executions in Beirut, and Yakuba's thoughts on what he'd say before being hanged himself, are from his oral testimony.

"I heard from a Syrian soldier": From Gamliel's fourteen-page report in the IDF archive.

"Love sanctified with blood": From Haim Gouri's "Song of Friendship," written amid the battles of 1948.

"Yigal Allon died without a homeland": The writer Amos Keinan in 1980, quoted in Shapira, *Yigal Allon, Native Son*.

The memo from September 16, 1948, announcing the Arab Section's move to military intelligence, is in the IDF archive.

The recruiting officer who identified Mizrahi names among new army draftees was Yosef Ben-Saadia, who spoke at the Arab Section reunion in 1985 (transcript in the Palmach archive).

"Yakuba has every authority to plan": Message from Arab Section headquarters to Beirut, December 24, 1948, 7:00 a.m., in the IDF archive.

"If I'm a prince and you're a prince": From Isaac's collection of Arabic sayings.

"If they'd accepted our plan when we were there": Yakuba speaking at the 1985 Arab Section reunion (transcript in the Palmach archive).

"When he talks about the period in Lebanon": Gamliel in his oral testimony.

Chapter 18: The Jewish State

"In the circles of students and intellectuals it is known": Report from the Arab Section (now Shin Mem 18), March 23, 1949, in IDF archives.

"And the land will grow quiet": From Nathan Alterman's poem "The Silver Platter," first published in the newspaper *Davar* on December 19, 1947.

"At the time I thought the war was over": From Yoram Kaniuk's memoir *Tashach* [1948] (Tel Aviv: Yediot Books and Hemed Books, 2010).

"The war was lost not to Jewish arms but to American dollars and Czech planes": From a report on Radio Damascus summarized in an Arabic press roundup by the Israeli Foreign Ministry (February 19–20, 1949), in the IDF archive.

Al-Qawuqji insisted that the fighters at the kibbutz were actually non-Jewish Russians: From Morris, *1948*.

"The Arab office in London has issued a statement": Report on Near East Arabic Radio in the Foreign Ministry press files (February 21–22, 1949).

"The battle could be resumed and the Jews routed": Ramallah Arabic Radio quoting an article from the newspaper *El-Ba'ath*, in the Foreign Ministry press file (February 1–2, 1949).

"The entire future of the Arab world": Radio Ramallah quoting an article from *El-Difaa*, in the Foreign Ministry press file (February 1–2, 1949).

"The Jews may believe they have won the war": Radio Ramallah announcer Azmi Nashashibi in the Foreign Ministry press file (February 17–18, 1949).

Emergency regulations were repealed: From a Foreign Ministry roundup of Israeli press articles, January 9, 1949, in the IDF archive.

The Assis juice factory opened a new production line. . . . A strike at the Ata textile factory was settled in favor of the workers: From a Jewish Agency pamphlet of news updates in Israel (March 12–18, 1949), in the IDF archive.

The Jaffa post office . . . now reopened . . . immigrants poured into the country through the Haifa port, thousands every week, nearly twenty-five-thousand in February alone, a quarter of a million that year: From a Foreign Ministry roundup of Israeli press articles, January 10, 1949, in the IDF archive.

The population grew by a percentage point every ten days: From the newspaper *Davar*, March 10, 1949, quoted in Foreign Ministry press roundup in IDF archive.

"The newspaper *Al-Nasr* reports": Arab Section report, February 1, 1949, in the IDF archive.

"The Jews of Damascus are concentrated in their neighborhood": Report in IDF archive, March 23, 1949. No source appears on the document, but it resembles other Arab Section reports in the same file.

"The lives of a million Jews in Muslim countries would be jeopardized": The head of Egypt's UN delegation speaking on November 24, 1947, cited in Morris, *1948*.

"Severe measures": Iraq's prime minister quoted in a British Foreign Office memo, September 12, 1947, cited in Morris, *1948*.

Syrian papers reported a freeze on Jewish bank accounts: From a summary of Syrian press reports in the Foreign Ministry files (February 22–23, 1949), in the IDF archive.

The Jews of Egypt were living in "constant fear and anxiety": From a Foreign Ministry report dated August 26, 1948, in the IDF archive.

These people will "never identify with the national mission": Gamliel quotes from this speech by Antoun Saadeh in his oral testimony.

"Palestine is our land, and the Jews are our dogs!": This chant, and other details of the Aleppo riots of November 30, 1947, are from my interviews in 2009–10 with Aleppo Jews who were there, including Rafi Sutton (the teenager mentioned here), Rabbi Isaac Tawil, Yosef Entebbe (the boy who slipped barefoot from a window), Batya Ron, and others. A fuller description of what happened that day appears in *The Aleppo Codex*.

Some of the points discussed in this chapter originated in an essay I wrote for *Mosaic* magazine, "Mizrahi Nation," June 1, 2014. For a critical work on the experience of Mizrahi Jews in Israel, see Yehouda Shenhav, *The Arab Jews: A Postcolonial Reading of Nationalism, Religion, and Ethnicity* (Stanford, CA: Stanford University Press, 2006). For an account of the exodus of the Jews of Arab lands, see Lyn Julius, *Uprooted: How 3000 Years of Jewish Civilisation in the Arab World Vanished Overnight* (London: Vallentine Mitchell, 2018).

"Perhaps these are not the Jews we would like to see coming here": The head of the Jewish Agency's Middle East department, Yaakov Zrubavel, speaking at a meeting of the Zionist Executive on June 5, 1949. Cited in Tom Segev, *1949: The First Israelis*, edited by Arlen Neal Weinstein (New York: Henry Holt, 1986).

"Will affect all aspects of life in the country": From a Foreign Ministry circular dated October 2, 1949, cited in Segev, *1949*.

The article by Aryeh Gelblum appeared in *Haaretz* on April 22, 1949, and is cited in Segev, *1949*. The response from Efraim Friedman appeared in *Haaretz* on May 8, 1949, found on microfilm at Israel's National Library in Jerusalem. Friedman, born in Holland, had spent four years as a Zionist emissary organizing Jewish emigration to Israel in North Africa.

Gamliel's insights into the cultural, religious, and political life of the country, the quote from his 1944 letter, and the description of the incident at the Tulkarm train station are from his oral testimony.

I owe the observation about the absence of Ashkenazi artists on the most played list to *Yediot Ahronot* reporter Amihai Atali, who tweeted the list (of fifteen songs in the preceding Hebrew calendar year, published in the same paper) on September 3, 2017.

"Sometimes imagination can play really dirty tricks": From Romain Gary, *The Kites*, translated by Miranda Richmond Mouillot (New York: New Directions, 2017).

Chapter 19: Georgette

The descriptions of Isaac's time in Beirut, and of Georgette, are from my interviews with Isaac.

The photographs in this chapter appear courtesy of the Palmach photo archive.

Yakuba's memory of Marie appears in his oral testimony. Gamliel's memory of his business associate's sister appears in his oral testimony.

Details of the affair of Uri Yisrael and other Shin Bet agents who married Arab women were reported by Or Heller in a documentary for Israel's Channel 10 TV (September 6, 2015). The journalist who termed this "an affair the Shin Bet would rather forget" is Marina Golan.

"They divided us into couples and started training us": Esther Yemini, quoted in Dror's official history.

"To my dear Havakuk, much peace!": Message from Arab Section headquarters to Beirut, December 6, 1949, 3:15 p.m., in the IDF archive.

"The press announces that the [Arab] League won't meet soon": Arab Section report, January 15, 1949, in IDF archive.

Hand-drawn maps of airports . . . and of the piers at Port Said in Egypt . . . sketches of Egyptian army uniforms . . . the symbol of the Syrian Third Regiment: From intelligence reports in the IDF archive.

The departure of the Egyptian ship *Skara*: Arab Section report, March 6, 1949, in the IDF archive.

Gamliel bought two scholarly books on the rise in pan-Arab sentiment: Mentioned in Gamliel's fourteen-page report in the IDF archive.

"At the workshop of Abd el-Razek Habib": Intelligence report, March 1, 1949, in the IDF archive.

In Syria the regime outlawed the sale of maps for security reasons: Arab Section report, March 6, 1949, in the IDF archive.

The Syrians had placed an order with Tito Bolo: Intelligence report, February 16, 1949, in the IDF archive.

Lebanese authorities were getting between fifty and sixty emigration requests every day . . . "the irreversible collapse of the standing of Christians in Lebanon": From a Foreign Ministry report (August 1948) in the IDF archive.

"A private guy, a good-looking guy, a lovely guy. Not arrogant": From Yakuba's oral testimony.

Another proposal was for the assassination of the Lebanese prime minister: From my interviews with Isaac, also described in Gamliel's published account.

Isaac's description of the run-in with the Beirut police is from my interviews with him.

"That's when I learned the lesson": From Isaac's book with Rafi Sutton.

"She fell in love with him": From Gamliel's published account.

"Our situation is dire. Isaac Shoshan's girl followed us": From a message from Beirut to Arab Section headquarters, April 25, 1950, in the memoir by Yehoshua Kedem (Mizrahi), *Ha-mistaarev ha-acharon be-levanon* [The last undercover Arab agent in Lebanon: From Damascus to Ramat Hasharon], self-published in 2013. I interviewed Yehoshua Mizrahi (who later took the Hebrew family name Kedem) in Ramat Hasharon in February 2016.

"He's a liar, a betrayer": From Gamliel's oral testimony.

"To the one who ruined my life": From Gamliel's published account.

The story of Yussef Shufani, reported by Ben Shani and Efrat Lechter, was broadcast on Israeli Channel 2 TV's investigative program *Uvda* on April 8, 2013.

Chapter 20: The Redhead

The two agents dispatched on May 3, 1949, were Yaakov Bokai and Efraim Efraim. (It was not unheard of for Middle Eastern Jews to have the same first name and family name.) My description of their infiltration into Jordan (officially designated Operation Goshen) relies in large part on Gamliel's published account and on the memoir by Yehoshua Kedem (Mizrahi), with additional detail from Eliyahu Rika's memoir *Parpar Ha-shachar*, my interviews with Isaac, and Yakuba's oral testimony. In describing this episode in his book, Gamliel quotes extensively from sources he identifies as "File 50" and "File 51" at the IDF archive, but there are no files corresponding to those numbers, possibly because of a reorganization of the archive since Gamliel did his research in the late 1990s. It is also possible that this material retains a level of classification that would have allowed Gamliel, a former intelligence operative, to view it, but not a researcher without security clearance. The same may be true of Kedem (Mizrahi), who cites times, dates, and a report from Efraim that did not appear in the files made available to me; hence my use of citations from their books when necessary in this chapter, rather than of the primary sources.

The photograph of Bokai and friends is from the Palmach archive. Yehoshua Kedem (Mizrahi) is standing at right.

"Our two friends have crossed the border": Message from headquarters to Beirut, May 3, 1949, File 50 at the IDF archive, cited in Gamliel's published account.

"A report has been published in Beirut of the arrest of two Jews": Message from Gamliel to headquarters, May 11, 1949, in File 51 at the IDF archive, cited in Gamliel's published account.

One paper was saying "two Arabs" caught during a POW exchange: *Al Ha-Mishmar*, May 10, 1949, in Gamliel's published account.

"Cancel your trip and do not go to the *poste restante*": Message from headquarters to Gamliel, date unclear, in File 51 at the IDF archive, cited in Gamliel's published account.

"They knew our addresses": From Yakuba's oral testimony.

"In wake of the arrest of our two comrades in Transjordan": Message from headquarters, May 12, 1949, cited in Gamliel's published account.

Efraim's account of what happened appears in a report he wrote afterward, quoted in full in the memoir by Kedem (Mizrahi). The report is undated but presumably dates to midsummer 1949. Efraim gives the date of his return to Israel as July 20. Details of Efraim's agitated mental state are from descriptions of the episode by the other agents, including Yakuba in his oral testimony, Gamliel in his published account, and Isaac in his interviews with me.

"It's a basic error to induct a redhead into the Black Section": From Rika's memoir *Parpar Ha-shachar*. In my 2019 interview with Rika, he told me that the doomed agent sensed the problem but never said anything to his commanders: "He wasn't brave enough to tell them he wasn't right for the job."

"I stayed in Amman for a week" and "They are not willing to live in barren Transjordan": From Gamliel's published account.

Efraim's return to Israel is described in Yakuba's oral testimony.

Bokai's British ID card identifying him as Najeeb Ibrahim Hamouda appears courtesy of the Palmach photo archive.

The visit to Jerusalem was described in Isaac's interviews with me, and in Gamliel's oral testimony and published account.

An identical Hebrew version of Bokai's letter appears in the books by Mizrahi and Gamliel. According to Yaron Behar, an expert on the early Arab Section, this version was a translation by Sam'an made immediately after the arrival of the letter in Arabic in August 1949. I could find no trace of the original letter. According to Gamliel, the released prisoner who brought the letter from Jordan was Hassan Ibrahim Ali, a Palestinian Arab from the West Bank town of Silwad.

The Israeli files give the date of Bokai's execution in Amman as August 2, 1949.

Chapter 21: Home

Isaac, Havakuk, and Shimon Horesh were extracted on April 19, 1950, according to Gamliel's account. Yakuba's oral testimony doesn't give a date for his return to Israel, but it seems to have been a few months earlier. Gamliel returned to Israel in late June or early July, according to his oral testimony. The agent Shaul Carmeli ("Tawfiq") had returned the previous year (on June 8, 1949, according to documents in the IDF archive), crossing the border overland.

The story about the old man who visited the Beirut kiosk is from Isaac's interviews with me.

The description of Isaac's extraction from the beach at Ouzai along with Havakuk and Shimon is from Isaac's interviews with me.

Gamliel's account of how he joined the Mossad is from his oral testimony. He served from 1952 to 1964.

"Gamliel was known in the intelligence community as one of Israel's most successful agents": The historian Meir Pa'il in an obituary for Gamliel by Oded Shalom, *Yediot Ahronot*, July 17, 2002.

Epilogue

Another old spy I know watched Isaac debrief an agent: This is Rafi Sutton, who described Isaac to me in one of our many conversations, and described watching him work in the book they wrote together in 1990.

Isaac's description of his return to Haifa is from his interviews with me.

ACKNOWLEDGMENTS

I'm grateful to my editor, Amy Gash, for her superior insight and for agreeing to follow me down another Middle Eastern rabbit hole; to the staff at Algonquin Books; to my agent Deborah Harris; to my Canadian publisher, Doug Pepper of Penguin Random House Canada; and to Felicia Herman, the members of Natan, and the Jewish Book Council for a generous vote of confidence. For reading the manuscript and offering advice, thanks to Mitch Ginsburg, Benjamin Balint, George Eltman, SS, George Deek, and Diaa El Radwa Hadid; to my sister, Sarah Sorek; and to my parents, Imogene and Raphael Friedman. Thanks to Rafi Sutton for introducing me to the world of Israel's first spies (and to Isaac Shoshan); to Yehonatan Gorenberg for Arabic assistance; and to David Bezmozgis for his expertise on Russian curses. I owe special gratitude to the historian Benny Morris, who took the time to read an early draft and set me straight on a few points; and to Yaron Behar, scholar of the early days of Israeli intelligence, who patiently answered my questions when I still knew close to nothing. Thanks to George Rohr and the Rohr family, whose support for my first book has helped me write two more. And thanks to my wife, Naama, and our children Aviv, Michael, Tamar, and Asaf, who've spent the last few years living with the Arab Section.

My research relied on invaluable Israeli libraries and archives, on their helpful staffers (Eldad Harouvi of the Palmach archive,

IDF archivist Yifat Arnon, and others), and on the many who took the time to speak to me. Too numerous to list here, they appear in the source notes. This book wouldn't have been possible without them. Above all, thanks to Isaac Shoshan for his time and his stories.

Of the four characters at the center of this book, three grew old in the country they helped create. One didn't: Havakuk, the watcher son of Yona and Yosef Cohen, born in Yemen in 1927, killed in December 1951 on Israel's desert border with Jordan. He was twenty-four. Besides the enduring affection of those who knew him, and a few intelligence reports testifying to a perceptive and sensitive soul, Havakuk left nearly nothing behind. This book is dedicated to him.

QUESTIONS FOR DISCUSSION

1. What did you learn from reading this book? What surprised you?

2. Isaac Shoshan started life as Zaki Shasho, and spent years as Abdul Karim Muhammad Sidki. Each name reflects different experiences, but all of those experiences were real. So what is his "real" identity? What does it mean to build an identity?

3. The agents underwent training in Arab culture to become *mista'arvim*, or "ones who become like Arabs." But Friedman writes, "Something complicated was happening in that tent . . . Who were these men? They were certainly not Muslims, which is why they had to learn Islam. But were they Arabs? They would have said no, and most Arabs would have said no. But they were native to the Arab world—as native as Arabs. If the key to belonging to the Arab nation was the Arabic language, as the Arab nationalists claimed, they were inside. So were they really 'becoming like Arabs'? Or were they already Arabs?" (p. 58). What do you think? Were these Mizrahi Jews Arab?

4. Why is the story of the Arab Section important to tell? There were plenty of Jewish units fighting in the War of Independence whose individual stories are not publicly known; why did Friedman choose this group to write about?

5. Friedman quotes Israeli writer Yonatan Ben-Nahum, who writes that for the Jews in the time of British Mandate Palestine, "'ethnic impersonation isn't a military doctrine used by sophisticated generals intent on victory, but the survival method of a persecuted wanderer who concealed his origins to save his life'" (p. 96). What do you think of this statement? Do you agree? Is it still relevant today? Is it true everywhere? Do you think the idea is specific to Jews or to any minority?

6. When you think of Israel, do you think of it as a Western-influenced country or a Middle Eastern one? In what ways? Why does it matter that, as of 2017, all of the top 15 pop songs in Israel were from Mizrahi artists (p. 171)? What does that say about Israel today, and how does it change our understanding of the past and present of the country, and of its relationship to its neighbors? Given that fully half the Jews in Israel (p. 169) have roots in the Islamic world, how would you change your narrative of the State of Israel?

7. Think of the title of the book. What does it mean and how does it apply to the Arab Section's work in 1948–49? How do you think it felt to risk your life as a spy for a country whose very existence was in question as you performed your covert missions?

8. The book ends with the story of the redhead, which only peripherally mentions the four main characters. Why do you think Friedman chose to include that section? How did it affect our spies? Did it shape the way you think about their stories?

9. What were the spies' attitudes toward the Arabs around them and the neighboring Arab countries? How did the story of the old man whose sons were mechanics (p. 208) fit into the spies' outlook? Friedman writes that this story seemed different from the others Isaac had told him (p. 209). Why do you think that is?

10. Yakuba and Gamliel differed on what they believed the job of an Arab Section spy to be: Gamliel saw it as an intellectual task that required observation and patience, while Yakuba was more interested in sabotage. Do you agree more with one or the other? Do you think the chosen strategy was the most effective?

11. In the introduction, Friedman discusses contemporary parallels to the "great Jewish exodus from the Arab world" (p. xv): "people making desperate escapes across the Mediterranean, washing up on Greek beaches . . . people who think or act differently and don't have a tribe that can protect them. The hatred of people who aren't like you, the idea that something will be solved if only such people can be made to disappear—this sometimes starts with Jews but tends not to end there." What do you think of this idea? What can the story of the spies teach us about the history, and the present, of the Middle East?

12. The story of the spies is the story of the humble beginnings of Israeli intelligence and the Mossad, which is now a powerful, sophisticated force. Did the origin story surprise you at all—how hardscrabble it was, who was part of it, what their initial missions were?

13. The European Jews who formed the core of the leadership of Israel for decades—from the pre-State period almost to the current moment—did not know what to make of Middle Eastern Jews like the spies; they looked different from the Jews they knew, spoke different languages, ate different foods, and had a different mentality. Yet it was precisely these differences that made the spies so valuable to the Arab Section, enabling them to blend in. What do you think motivated the spies to risk their lives for a country that did not understand them and in many ways did not accept them? Would you have done the same?

Discussion questions appear courtesy of the Jewish Book Council and Natan Fund.

MARY ANDERSON

Matti Friedman's 2016 book *Pumpkinflowers* was chosen as a *New York Times* Notable Book and as one of Amazon's 10 Best Books of the Year. It was selected as one of the year's best by *Booklist*, *Mother Jones*, *Foreign Affairs*, the *National Post*, and the *Globe and Mail*. His first book, *The Aleppo Codex*, won the 2014 Sami Rohr Prize and the American Library Association's Sophie Brody Medal. A contributor to the *New York Times* opinion page, Friedman has reported from Israel, Lebanon, Morocco, Moscow, the Caucasus, and Washington, DC, and his writing has appeared in publications such as the *Wall Street Journal*, the *Atlantic*, and the *Washington Post*. Friedman grew up in Toronto and now lives with his family in Jerusalem.